Building an Outreach Ministry to Your Community

How to Grow Your Church
by Ministering to People

Tyrone Barnette

THOM S. RAINER, SERIES EDITOR

TYNDALE
MOMENTUM®

A Tyndale nonfiction imprint

Visit Tyndale online at tyndale.com.

Visit Tyndale Momentum online at tyndalemomentum.com.

Tyndale, Tyndale's quill logo, *Tyndale Momentum*, and the Tyndale Momentum logo are registered trademarks of Tyndale House Ministries. Tyndale Momentum is a nonfiction imprint of Tyndale House Publishers, Carol Stream, Illinois.

Building an Outreach Ministry to Your Community: How to Grow Your Church by Ministering to People

For information about special discounts for bulk purchases, please contact Tyndale House Publishers at csresponse@tyndale.com, or call 1-855-277-9400.

Library of Congress Cataloging-in-Publication Data

A catalog record for this book is available from the Library of Congress.

ISBN 978-1-4964-6702-7

Printed in the United States of America

29	28	27	26	25	24	23
7	6	5	4	3	2	1

Contents

Outreach Is Our Family Business

My preoccupation with outreach started when I was nine years old. I awoke one morning to the sound of weeping in the kitchen. I crept toward the hallway and peeked around the corner to see my mother and father seated at the table with a young woman. She was the source of the sobbing, and I noticed she was holding a napkin stained with blood.

For a few moments, I listened undetected to their conversation and discovered that she had been beaten by her husband or boyfriend and had run to our house seeking my parents' protection and support. My parents were known in the community for their openhanded love and compassion for anyone in need. I recall feeling proud to be their son and that our home was seen as a safe place for anyone needing comfort.

Throughout my life, my family has modeled sacrificial love, especially to the marginalized in society. I grew up watching my mother volunteer at women's shelters in our small town in North Carolina. Even into her seventies, she still works with patients experiencing memory loss. My father and grandfather hired men who were suffering with alcohol addiction as day laborers in their construction business. My maternal grandparents employed young men and women who needed a job to work on their farm and gave them a place to sleep for weeks until they could fend for themselves.

My family members weren't motivated by political or social ideology. They gave themselves away unselfishly because they had internalized and responded to the call of God to reach their community and share the love of Christ. They were inspired by our little church and the faithful preaching of pastors who continually challenged us to go and make disciples for Christ. Despite limited resources and a lack of formal ministerial training, they did many other magnanimous things as well.

Somehow I always knew that their example would inspire and inform my own life's mission. You could say that helping others is our family business.

Outreach: It's Your Family Business Too

If I may be so bold: Outreach should be *your* family business as well. The command to "go and make disciples" (Matthew 28:19) was not just a directive for the original disciples or for today's clergy. It is a mandate for every one of us to use our lives as conduits of God's grace to those in need. Christ intends for us to invest whatever gifts or opportunities he has granted us to advance his Kingdom. We are called to reach every tribe, every tongue, every nation—starting with our own neighborhoods.

Many books have been written to encourage Christians to reach their communities through evangelism. They suggest dozens of ideas and concepts suited to their particular setting. However, I've learned that successful strategies in New York may not translate well in Kentucky. A community cookout that works in Texas may not have the same success on a beach in California—though I don't know many people who can resist a good barbecue. Outreach and evangelism are not cookie-cutter endeavors. From church to church, each expression will look different.

In these pages you will not find geographic, racial, or cultural ideas that work only in a specific context. We will explore God's mandate to reach the world by using time-tested, biblically supported principles that any church—of any size, location, or age—can immediately use.

I will attempt to challenge the way we think about outreach. I will question how we view our church, its leaders, and the members' responsibility to the Great Commission. We'll discover new ways to view our communities—especially the difficult, hard-to-reach areas—and prayerfully learn that God can take the little we have and multiply his Kingdom beyond our wildest dreams.

The church is the only hope for redeeming and renewing the world. It has its flaws and imperfections in how it proclaims the power of God and carries out his mission on earth; but Jesus loves the church—it's his body—and he has equipped his church with not only defensive spiritual armor, but with the powerful offensive weapon of his Word to challenge the very powers of hell (Ephesians 6:14-17). The church's mission is not to just hold our ground and march in place, but to take back territory that is occupied by the enemy. Christ calls us to work in partnership with him to transform any person or any culture, and to confront any issue that prevents humanity from reflecting God's glory.

I've chosen to frame our discourse by using the one miracle (other than the resurrection of Jesus) recorded in all four Gospels: the feeding of the five thousand. I don't believe it's a coincidence that Matthew, Mark, Luke, and John all include this event in their accounts of the life of Jesus.

This significant miracle gives us insight into how we can advance our evangelistic mandate and execute dynamic outreach work now and throughout time. It shows us how to use the resources we have by relying on Christ's power to multiply our efforts. Christ's example teaches us that any church or individual—no matter their age, background, or environment—can meet the demands of a hungry world and fill people with the life-giving bread he offers.

People are hungry. The majority are starving. Sadly, they crave things from this world's system that will never satisfy and only leave them thirsting for something more. The church of Jesus Christ has been equipped with the sustenance they need. The gospel will quench their thirst and gratify their hunger. But we must believe that what we have to offer is enough and sufficient.

When I was growing up, my family didn't have a lot of the material wealth this world relies on to address human needs. My parents believed that what Christ had put in their hands was sufficient. And they were not afraid to give their best to Christ and trust that he could cause it to flourish if they would simply release it.

For three decades I have pastored one church. In that time, I have attempted to live out the principles that transformed a gathering of fourteen adults in my living room into a congregation of more than three thousand ordinary men, women, and young people who have witnessed the miracle of multiplication, not only in our church but in our community and around the world as well. We have not mastered outreach—we are certainly still learning; but I'm grateful to God for entrusting to me one of the most loving and forgiving communities of believers to join me in distributing Christ's life-giving bread.

I long for your church to become a place of refuge like my childhood home. I pray that your church will stand as a beacon of hope for all who long for relief and rescue from the darkness that envelops far too many. I also pray that you will experience the phenomenal release of God's power in your life as Christ reveals the miracle of multiplication.

How the Book Is Organized

I got the idea for a book about the miracle of the feeding of the five thousand the last time I visited Israel. As I sat on the Bethsaida hillside that is believed to be where this miracle occurred, I visualized Jesus, the disciples, and the horde of humanity assembled there. I saw a clear picture of how God wants to use us, his church, to respond to the hunger that swells up from deep within the souls of people in our community. I made an immediate connection between how Jesus responded to their needs and how we must respond today.

In Part I, we will look at specific Scripture verses explaining what Jesus did while performing this miracle. I will identify principles of outreach that can help us in our quest to reach our communities with the living bread of the gospel. At the end of each chapter, brief prayers or exercises will help you integrate the lesson into your own life and ministry.

Part II consists of practical ways that a church or individual can apply these principles in their community. Since the COVID-19 pandemic, the world has radically changed. Patterns of church attendance, giving, discipleship, and worship look different today than at the beginning of 2020. Yet God still expects us to reach the world and fulfill our Great Commission directive from Matthew 28:19-20. I'll offer suggestions to help you pivot into this "new normal."

At the ends of certain chapters, you will find interviews with critical thinkers and gospel practitioners who share their insights concerning outreach and evangelism. You will glean wisdom from a professor, a church planter, pastors, and parachurch practitioners with decades of experience.

My hope is that this book will renew your passion for ministry and inspire you and your church to pursue transformative engagement with your community. I'm excited to see how the church and community can intersect today in what I am calling a technological reformation. Let's embrace these technological and cultural changes and emerge stronger than ever to deliver the Bread of Life to spiritually starving people who need to be fed.

Jesus Feeds Five Thousand

As soon as Jesus heard the news, he left in a boat to a remote area to be alone. But the crowds heard where he was headed and followed on foot from many towns. Jesus saw the huge crowd as he stepped from the boat, and he had compassion on them and healed their sick.

That evening the disciples came to him and said, "This is a remote place, and it's already getting late. Send the crowds away so they can go to the villages and buy food for themselves."

But Jesus said, "That isn't necessary—you feed them."

"But we have only five loaves of bread and two fish!" they answered.

"Bring them here," he said. Then he told the people to sit down on the grass. Jesus took the five loaves and two fish, looked up toward heaven, and blessed them. Then, breaking the loaves into pieces, he gave the bread to the disciples, who distributed it to the people. They all ate as much as they wanted, and afterward, the disciples picked up twelve baskets of leftovers. About 5,000 men were fed that day, in addition to all the women and children!

MATTHEW 14:13-21

PART I

HOW JESUS REACHED HIS COMMUNITY

1

Ministry Can Happen Anywhere

As soon as Jesus heard the news, he left in a boat
to a remote area to be alone. But the crowds heard where
he was headed and followed on foot from many towns.
MATTHEW 14:13 (EMPHASIS ADDED)

I RECENTLY HAD A CONVERSATION with a pastor of a small rural church in South Georgia. His church was experiencing what he described as a season of coasting along and drifting. He attributed this melancholy ministry mood to the fact that the church was in a small town with one high school, one McDonald's, and a short drive to the nearest Walmart in the next town. He had resigned himself to believing that the church would not grow because it had been planted years ago in a deserted place that provided few opportunities for innovative ministry to be established.

Not long after that conversation, I spoke to another pastor who ministered in the inner city of Indianapolis, Indiana. He had a similar complaint that it was nearly impossible to grow the church because it was in the poorest section of the city and had an out-of-control crime rate that hindered his ability to make a significant impact. He longed to convince the church to sell its property and move out to the suburbs near a popular mall so the church could finally grow.

Sadly, this is the attitude of many leaders. They follow the advice of real estate agents who say the most important factor in finding a good home is location, location, location. This belief is pervasive among church leadership, regardless of the church setting. I have heard this sentiment from leaders and congregants alike whether the church is in a rural area, in a population-rich urban center, or in a growing suburban community with homes valued well above the national average.

Many have subscribed to the notion that "we can't grow here" because the location is not picture-perfect. They envy the ministry in the next town or state that seems to be in the ideal community. They imagine what it would be like to have a community with better demographics, newly constructed homes, and modern infrastructure. And those churches in the model communities with all the cutting-edge advantages are frustrated because they coexist with disengaged residents who have no time for, or interest in, church. These suburban pastors yearn for smaller places where true community and relationships can form like in a Norman Rockwell painting.

But Jesus shows us in the feeding of the five thousand that ministry can bloom and blossom anywhere. Even in a solitary and remote place.

Luke's account prefaces the miracle by stating that Jesus "slipped quietly away with [the disciples] toward the town of Bethsaida" (Luke 9:10). He was seeking out a place for quiet rest. This miracle happens in an area that should not have experienced this measure of success. There were no grocery stores, no gardens or farms, and no access to supplies of any kind. Yet, Jesus feeds five thousand plus without calling Uber Eats or DoorDash or relocating anyone.

Now there are legitimate reasons to relocate a church once it has outgrown the current space, or there's a desire to reach a new target group, or the area has become too industrial or commercial. However, in my experience, though the motive to move may be reasonable, many churches move without fully exploring the opportunities at their current facility.

Expanding to two or three worship times could provide the necessary growth potential without a physical move. Other options include going multisite or starting a weeknight service, as many churches now do. Adding a weeknight service has become a viable alternative to relocation for some ministries in communities where many residents work on the weekends. A weeknight worship service also accommodates people who may be traveling that weekend.

Ministry can happen anywhere. Take time to examine your neighborhood with fresh eyes, and allow God to show you opportunities that await your discovery. When churches are inwardly focused, they almost completely prioritize keeping the current members satisfied and put little effort into reaching new people who are just outside the doors.

As Tony Morgan writes in his book *The Unstuck Church*, "Many churches don't have a strategy; they have mission statements. They know why they exist. They have a vision. They know where they believe God has called their ministries to be in the future. What they don't have is a strategy on how to accomplish that vision. Without a clearly defined strategy, churches gravitate toward what they've always done. . . . With every iteration of the vision, more things are added, but nothing is ever subtracted."[1]

So the answer for church health and growth may not be adding new programs or relocating to what appears to be greener pastures on the other side of town. Instead, it may be to clarify a strategy for how the church in its current state and location can reach its community and become more outwardly focused. This might require eliminating some existing programs to have energy and margin to connect with the neighbors and new people groups right where the church is located.

Don't consider a move until you have explored and exhausted every opportunity to evangelize the community your church is in. Jesus said in John 4:35, "Wake up and look around. The fields are already ripe for harvest." Ministry can happen anywhere!

Thank God for where he has called you. Express your gratitude, apprehension, and anticipation for what he will do with you there. Pray for your church that it will take full advantage of the opportunities that have been and will be presented to it over the next year.

2

Attracting a Crowd

*The crowds heard where [Jesus] was headed
and followed on foot from many towns.*

MATTHEW 14:13

AT A LEADERSHIP CONFERENCE YEARS AGO, I heard John Maxwell say, "If you think you're leading but no one is following, you're just taking a walk." Leaders create followers, inspiring them to action by what they say and the compelling vision they promote.

In the text, men, women, and children are following Jesus on foot. They left their homes and traveled miles just to receive more of his teaching and to witness the power of his ministry. I firmly believe that every church and every believer should have this kind of impact. There should be something unique and special about our ministry and mission that attracts people.

Paul said, "Follow me as I follow Christ" (1 Corinthians 11:1, MEV). It is essential that we are being led by the Lord and bringing people to Christ, and that they are not drawn primarily by our personality, programs, or charisma. But we must have something compelling that bubbles up from within us and draws people to our ministry and message.

Discovering what makes our ministry attractive is one of the keys that unlocks our full potential to reach our community for Christ. Sadly, many congregations struggle to define what is distinctive and exceptional about their church. Instead of being original, many churches simply shape themselves into cheap copies of what other churches are doing. Church conferences and seminars are notorious for packaging concepts and systems in neatly organized steps that attendees are encouraged to try out in their places of worship—only to discover that, just as David was unable to wear Saul's armor when he fought Goliath, the system doesn't fit the anointing God has given them.

God has placed you and your church in that particular neighborhood to reach that specific population. Your church is equipped with the exact mixture of members and ministerial acumen that is needed to meet the concerns of the particular demographic you are called to. When you do the work, people will be drawn to receive the rich deposits of grace God has placed within you and your church.

Your church may be equipped with members who are excellent in counseling and have spiritual gifts of mercy, hospitality, and discernment. So perhaps God's plan is for yours to be the church with several support groups or a counseling center for the community. Another ministry may be full of teachers, so it may be called to start a school or have a dynamic after-school program for various ages. A different church may be stocked with talented singers, skillful craftsmen, or amazing cooks who can conduct clinics or workshops for the community.

The discovery that we were attracting many people who had struggled with substance abuse awakened me to God's desire that our church become known as a recovery center. Over the years, we have seen thousands of people come through our ministry and find deliverance from drugs and alcohol. We are proud to be known as the church that welcomes those struggling with addictions. It's who we are and it's who we attract.

People from all over metro Atlanta drive miles to our church because they know it is a safe place to lay down their burdens and reveal their pain. Our reputation as a safe place for recovery attracts not only those who face the challenge of addiction, but also those who want to help them recover. Doctors, social workers, and police officers have joined our church in significant numbers because they want to use their special training to help us disciple persons in distress.

God is presently sending creatives and gifted artists from all fields to our campus. We have embraced the arts in our worship services with a high emphasis on drama, dance, and singing. This focus appeals to people talented in theater, costume design, lighting, and vocal and instrumental music. Each year we produce several original dramas that coincide with our sermon series, organize dance troupes for ages six to eighty-six, and teach technical theater classes (sound, lighting, staging) in the local high school.

Each person and church is uniquely gifted with a special mix of talents and life experiences that attract a certain demographic of people. I tell church leaders all the time that "your ministry is in your mess." Your purpose resides in your pain. The ways God has shaped you and brought you through certain episodes has equipped you to be a beacon of hope to someone who needs to reap from the garden you have watered with your tears.

In the miracle story of feeding the five thousand, Jesus had just heard that John the Baptist had been beheaded. He withdrew to this solitary place because he was in pain after hearing the news of John's murder. I like to think that Jesus' familiarity with pain was one of the chief reasons crowds were drawn to him. He could relate, and he ministered to them out of his own grief. Isaiah 53:3 reminds us that Jesus was "a man of sorrows, acquainted with deepest grief." No wonder the hurting and desolate found comfort around him.

This is why it is important for you as an individual and for your congregation to be aware of your own peculiar sensitivity and ability to assist people in pain.

What distinctive gifts, talents, skills, or abilities does your ministry possess that God uses to bring people to your ministry? This principle of attraction is often overlooked in discussions on evangelism and outreach, but God uses our stories to introduce others to his story.

Dr. Reggie Ogea Interview

*Reggie Ogea's forty-two years of vocational ministry include
pastoring three churches, serving as director of missions for
the Northshore Baptist Association in southeast Louisiana, and
teaching for eighteen years at New Orleans Baptist Theological
Seminary. With his experience in strategic planning and
denominational systems analysis, he has assisted denominational
associations and state conventions as a consultant and conference
leader. He has also used his skills in conflict resolution, church
revitalization, and strategic leadership to serve various churches
as an interim pastor, strategic planner, and conflict mediator.*

Tyrone Barnette

How are seminaries and Bible colleges training students today
in evangelism and outreach? Has there been a change in their
approach over the last twenty years?

Dr. Reggie Ogea

I can't speak about other seminaries, but I don't think that
there's been a change in our approach. Especially at the
New Orleans Baptist Theological Seminary, where I teach, we
have always been an evangelistic seminary. We've always had
evangelism as one of our core values. And we believe pastors,
especially, ought to not only be trained, but they should be
instructed and given the necessary tools to do evangelism. We're
one of the only denominational seminaries that require our
students to participate in knowing how to share their faith. It's a
part of their assignments. It's not optional. So, no, I don't think it
has changed in twenty years.

But I will say this, we have enough issues in our own
SBC seminaries and our own denomination to know that our

evangelistic profiles have declined, and our churches are not reaching as many people, and we're not baptizing as many people as we did twenty years ago.

We've been in decline for twenty years or more, and that ought to be a grave concern to us all. But it just doesn't seem like we're taking any hard-core initiatives to turn it around. I mean, we're trying a few things. But until the pastor assumes the role of also being an evangelist, we won't make much headway.

In 2 Timothy 4:5 [NASB], Paul simply said to Timothy, "Do the work of an evangelist, fulfill your ministry." I take the Scriptures literally, as you know, and I think Paul is saying you can't fulfill your ministry calling as a pastor unless you are doing the work of an evangelist. If we as pastors got serious about evangelism, I believe we could turn it around ourselves and not depend on anybody else.

At New Orleans Seminary, we had a professor who did a lot of research in the area of pastoral ministry and evangelism. He did an in-house study and presented his findings to the faculty. I recall he said that if every pastor personally reached one more person with the gospel than he had the previous year, we would double our baptismal rate across the Southern Baptist Convention in one year. Well, again, what that says is that we the pastors are not doing what we need to be doing, or else we wouldn't be in such a decline.

Tyrone Barnette

What are some trends you are seeing implemented by churches today to reach our communities? Any innovative ones?

Dr. Reggie Ogea

I wouldn't call it a trend, maybe a different strategy or a different way of doing evangelism than what we could do in the past. It's not like it used to be when we went door-to-door, although there's still plenty of research that indicates door-to-door evangelism still works.

But the strategies for evangelism that are biblically based are no different in the twenty-first century than they were in the first century. The Great Commission is still for every individual Christian. Jesus said to his disciples, "Wait for the infilling and the empowering of the Holy Spirit. You go be my witnesses, you go evangelize, and make disciples of all the ethnos wherever God sends you" [Acts 1:8, paraphrased]. They had no idea when Jesus gave them that commission that he was going to force them out of Jerusalem. But they took it seriously, because everywhere they were scattered they began to evangelize. So they got it.

The problem now is we *don't* get it. Here's the other sad thing: The Lord has brought the ethnos of the world to us. I live in New Orleans; you live in Atlanta. Could there be any two more diverse, multiethnic, and multicultural cities than those two? God doesn't have to scatter us for us to evangelize like they did in the first century. He's brought the world to us. Christ has made it easier for us than he did for the first-century Christians. So what's up with what we're not doing?

Tyrone Barnette

Yeah, we've always been looking for the new cutting-edge strategy that is going to fix it all. Scripture gives us the blueprint. Our methods may have to adjust to culture, but the ultimate strategy is the same as in Acts 1:8.

How has the pandemic changed the church? I've been calling it a technological reformation. Today through technology, every local church can become a global church and reach the world through streaming and online ministry. Your thoughts?

Dr. Reggie Ogea

The global pandemic has created some new and different opportunities for us. Prior to the shutdown, most of our churches, especially our smaller churches, weren't serious about live streaming. We were only concerned with gathering for worship.

But all of a sudden, when we couldn't gather, we had to figure out how to do church outside the building. Quite quickly, the smaller churches I observed did better than some of the larger churches.

This change gave us a new opportunity, a new way of worshiping, and a new way of getting the gospel out. We found there were other people who now watch online. Now we've just added a different kind of folk to our prospect list. And now we've got to increase our technological acumen to get to know them and reach them, because it looks as if many of the people we once had are not coming back.

Those who are resistant to technology and online churches are going to have to embrace it as an accepted standard, a new protocol, and a way for us to function as the church. The ones who figure out how to do it more evangelistically are going to reap the outreach benefits.

Many churches will do okay for now, as long as the resources are still coming in. But when lower attendance starts to affect the offering, it's going to have a huge impact. Because when churches start having serious financial issues, you know as well as I do, that's when you get all kinds of conflict and struggles flashing up before you.

3

Embracing the Technological Reformation

The crowds heard where he was headed and
followed on foot from many towns.
MATTHEW 14:13 (EMPHASIS ADDED)

BACK IN THE LATE 1990s when the Internet was moving into mainstream America and expanding into the business and entertainment world, the church was slow to adopt it. I remember pastors preaching sermons about its dangers and the evil of the World Wide Web. It took a while for the church to realize that we needed to learn how to leverage this new technology for the furtherance of the gospel.

Sadly, I was one of those preachers who looked with suspicion at the Web's ability to do good. I prided myself on being a no-tech to low-tech type of guy. It took some time for me to warm to the abundant opportunities the Internet could provide.

We started with a very basic website that gave some general information on our church. I quickly found out that people were coming to our services because they first visited our website.

Members began sharing the website address with their friends and families, and within a short amount of time, we were holding three Sunday morning worship services and had become the ninety-third-fastest-growing church in America in 2004, according to *Outreach* magazine.

While we saw noteworthy success from our crude website, we didn't take advantage of it beyond just putting it up. Information was rarely updated, I seldom mentioned social media from the pulpit, we didn't post or blog, and we didn't use email or (later) text messaging to carry out a follow-up strategy with our members and visitors. The church kept growing due to our personal evangelism efforts in the community. But I have often wondered what we could have achieved if we had embraced the full capacity of the Internet as early adopters of the trend.

The pandemic of 2020 opened the eyes of every church around the world to the necessity of the Internet for effective twenty-first-century ministry. Without it, we could not have carried out our mission, kept our congregations connected, and supported our ministries financially.

Thankfully, we had implemented a full expansion of our online infrastructure and personnel two years before the pandemic hit. We hired full-time staff, upgraded our equipment and lighting, and began to move our church communications from paper to a digital format by using email and other technologies. So when the nation shut down in March 2020 and there were no in-person worship gatherings, we didn't miss a beat. We were able to help other churches navigate through that season and sustain their ministries. Years before the pandemic, we held classes to teach our senior adults how to access technology, use computers, send email, join Bible study chat rooms, and operate their smartphones.

If it weren't for God's grace and the Internet, we, along with every other church, would have been in a difficult spot. We would have lost touch with our members, hindering our ability to continue to serve our community, public schools, and strategic partners. The fellowship fabric we had sewn together could have been torn apart overnight, and it would have taken us years to reestablish it. Thankfully we had built a church that was not afraid to embrace technology.

Ministry leader Nona Jones warns that if the church does not learn to embrace technological advancements, we will be left behind (not a reference to the Rapture). She shared that pastors resisted the printing press centuries ago because they were fearful that people would not attend church and just read the sermon in print later. When radio and television came into the mainstream, pastors were against them for the same reasons. And today, many are apprehensive about online streaming and view it as a threat to our established church culture and traditions. Jones writes, "At every juncture of technological advancement, naysayers have resisted the change only to fall in line with it *after it was too late* and a new development was on the rise."[2] Churches are typically the last to adopt new innovations, and they lag far behind the rest of the culture.

The pandemic forced every church to at least try out social media for a few weeks and some for more than a year. My hope is that God allowed this to give us a taste of what is possible when we harness new technologies to reach the world with the gospel. We are going to have to think on-site and online simultaneously when we are planning our services, teaching our discipleship classes, and serving the community.

As of this writing, our church has more people connecting with us online than we have in live worship each Sunday. At first, I was frantically trying to get them back in the building. But I quickly realized that we were experiencing a paradigm shift in our church life. So now I no longer resist it. I've embraced it. Our staff and church family have embraced it. We see it as a tool God has given us and others to take his message much farther than out our front door and down the street.

Like Martin Luther in the 1500s, we are on the horizon of a reformation. His was theological. Ours is technological. We don't have to nail anything to a wooden door, as Luther did. We can just blog about it on our computers and smartphones and let the world know that the church of Jesus Christ is unleashed and is no longer bound by our buildings. I pray you join me and other churches as we cast a global vision to extend beyond our Jerusalem, surpassing Judea, far past Samaria, and toward the ends of the earth.

What are your thoughts concerning the impact of technology on your church? What are the benefits? What challenges do you foresee?

Ben McDonald Interview

Ben McDonald is the founder and leader of Be The Church, an online Christian community launched in January 2021. Along with his wife, Peeper, and a group of creatives, he developed a new church model focused on relationships, equipping and empowering people outside the traditional one-hour weekend service. Using technology and social media, they teach people how to put faith into action and be the church everywhere they go. His church movement is rapidly growing near Atlanta.

Tyrone Barnette

Tell me about your ministry.

Ben McDonald

At the start of the pandemic, one of the questions I felt that God really put on my heart was, How are we going to continue to fulfill the Great Commission if we're not able to gather in person? I began to wonder, have we allowed people to change the Great Commission to say, "Go into all the world and invite your friends to this building" so the pastor can preach to them, then hopefully a small group leader can teach them to obey, and hopefully somebody on staff can baptize them?

Versus really turning it into empowering every believer and ensuring that each member is responsible to go make disciples and to teach people to obey Jesus' teachings.

And so through that, I began to pray and engage in conversations and do studies and eventually formed our ministry called Be The Church. Be The Church is a digital church first and also meets once a month in person. Our whole goal is to equip and empower people to be the church every day, everywhere they go.

Studies show that the average person is connected to some

kind of technological resource seven plus hours a day in the US. Whether that's a phone, a tablet, a TV, or a computer, we depend on technology; we depend on digital to live our lives.

I love what Jesus says in Matthew 10:7: "*As you go*, proclaim this message: 'The kingdom of heaven has come near.'"[3] So . . .

as you go on Facebook, Instagram, or YouTube,

as you go to work or school,

as you're driving,

as you go, preach the gospel.

We have an incredible opportunity, because every person is a digital missionary, with the opportunity to go into the digital world and into social media, to have an impact in their spheres of influence. Maybe it's a short post, sharing a verse of the day, or recording a small video. Those are all tools and resources for sending believers into their digital communities and really feeding the thousands. Be The Church is all about equipping and empowering people to do that.

We're also collaborating with churches to maximize what they're doing in their buildings and taking that in a digital way to reach the thousands.

Attendance isn't fully back, you know. In some areas it's back to normal, but not everywhere yet. I think we can utilize our existing influence and begin to build on that influence by letting people see our lives, not just hear the message. That's really what Jesus was about. People didn't just hear about his message and miracles. They heard about the life he lived and the relationships he had, and the way he served the people he encountered.

Tyrone Barnette

That's a really good framework of *why* you do what you do. But how do you carry out your digital ministry and how should pastors be thinking digitally for their ministries?

Ben McDonald

People will check out your website and your online service before they come to the in-person service. It could be months of that. I think it starts with your Sunday message. You could utilize clips from Sunday or reshoot it specifically for social media. You could even come offstage and shoot a two- or three-minute synopsis of what you just preached.

Grow your influence by increasing your Facebook presence. Create some groups where you can connect with people. We utilize what we call a prayer room. Currently 360 people are actively engaged there—so that's a community. I'll post, "Here's something I'm struggling with" or "Here's something you can pray for me about," and other people comment and engage as well.

We created a digital Connect card for everyone who encounters us. As soon as they sign up for that list, they get an email telling them a little bit of our vision for the church and what we're doing. It tells them where we meet in person once a month and how to engage every week digitally. We also recommend past series, and they can find past messages on YouTube.

We let them know that we're here for them and praying for them, and we give them a number where they can text. If they need to talk with somebody or want to connect, we will respond. I think part of what people want is to be able to connect. They want to be able to touch Jesus, versus just hearing me preach. People want to know they can reach out to you. Some people have never had that personalized touch from anyone in their lives.

So, once we get their email, they're on our email list. At least weekly they'll get an email with an encouraging video, a message, or a connection opportunity. It could let them know what's coming up, or it could be a mission opportunity they can join.

Most people aren't going to walk in your doors and immediately be ready to serve on the worship team and commit to a couple of hours every week. But I'm bringing them into a Bible reading plan and eventually a digital discipleship course. And then they're committed for maybe seven weeks on a topic on lordship or repentance or the Holy Spirit's work in spiritual gifts.

We also connect them to relationships, which are so important in discipleship. We connect them to a coach, someone who can be in their lives and answer questions, who can facilitate discussion and really do the relational aspect of discipleship. They need their questions answered. They can watch the content anytime, but the relationship is really where the rubber meets the road. Again, the goal is to bring them closer and closer for influence and engagement, which leads to discipleship and (later) leadership.

Tyrone Barnette

What advice would you give to a church that is more accustomed to using traditional ministry methods? How can they embrace some of the concepts you've shared? What are some first steps to help them transition?

Ben McDonald

I would say that your congregation is already on social media. They already have a following who could help. Use those contacts to extend your sermon to a larger audience by having your congregation share your sermon with their connections.

Or what would it look like for your members to get a midweek post from you, reminding them of the message they resonated with on Sunday and how to put it into practice in their lives? I think maybe that'll be a game changer for a start.

Tyrone Barnette

How can churches connect with you?

Ben McDonald

They can find us at www.bethechurch.info on all the platforms.

4

Jesus Saw Their Pain

Jesus saw the huge crowd as he stepped from the boat,
and he had compassion on them and healed their sick.

MATTHEW 14:14

EACH WEEKDAY, I generally take the same route from my home to the church office, depending on Atlanta traffic. If you've driven through Atlanta, you know what I mean. I pass the usual gas stations, houses, and buildings that line the street. Typically, on an off-ramp just before the church, I would see the same homeless man standing at the stoplight asking for pocket change.

As I approached the intersection, I would secretly pray that the light would turn green so I wouldn't have to stop and participate in this man's daily ritual of seeking assistance. I felt guilty for my attitude, but I also felt justified at some level for not giving out change that would likely be used to buy alcohol.

Occasionally I would give him some change or an apple I had meant for my snack. But most days I was able to speed past, keeping my eyes straight forward with my hands gripping the steering wheel. Yet, more than a few times, I heard the Holy Spirit whisper to me as I made my way to the office up the street.

Did you see him?

I would give some excuse or mutter a remorseful prayer. But within seconds my thoughts would return to my responsibilities at the church God has called me to serve, and the stoplight panhandler was forgotten.

Everything changed one day when I stopped long enough to have a brief conversation with the man. The light changed fairly quickly and did not afford us a lot of time to talk, so I pulled over down the street and walked back across the overpass to continue our conversation. I reintroduced myself and reminded him that we had a church two blocks away, with food if he needed it. He knew of it and had taken advantage of it from time to time.

I started to leave, but then turned back to ask him, "Tell me about yourself. How did you get here?" He began to share his story and his long journey to living on the street and sleeping under the stars.

For the first time, I really *saw* him, and I wondered whether it was the first time anyone had *listened* to him as well. I discovered we were the same age—in fact, we shared a birthday. We'd had similar upbringings but had chosen different paths and different ways to deal with our pain.

I invited him to church, and he came the very next week. And he kept coming for the next few years, never missing a week. I watched him migrate from sitting in the back of the church to a place near the front. Eventually, he accepted Christ and became one of our most vocal worshipers and a faithful Sunday school attender. He was embraced by our entire congregation, and we loved him.

It took a while for him to accept our help in getting him off the street. Even after some of our members found him housing, for some time he reverted back and forth between both worlds. But one day I realized it had been months since I had seen him panhandling in the neighborhood.

To my delight, he had secured a job at a local department store and was working and earning a living with a new lease on life. I felt like a proud parent, a big brother, and a coach.

But my feelings of joy paled in comparison to his. By the power of the Holy Spirit and the love of a congregation who knew that nothing was impossible if we would just believe, he had fought off a lifetime of demons that had clung to him like glue. He is a trophy of grace. A diamond that reclaimed its shine.

I think about how his story might have gone if I hadn't taken the time to park my car along the curb and walk back to look him in the eye and let him know that I saw him. In every city and town in the country there are men and women who need us to give them the very things their life's choices or circumstances have taken away: dignity and respect.

Robert Lupton wrote a book that changed my life and how I engage with people on the street who struggle. In *Toxic Charity: How Churches and Charities Hurt Those They Help (And How to Reverse It)*, Lupton writes:

Effective service among the less privileged requires a significant degree of awareness and delicacy. Sometimes even the most innocent and well-meaning attempts to help, inflict pain. Made in the image of God, we are created with intrinsic worth. And anything that erodes a rightful sense of pride and self-respect diminishes that image. At best we are fragile, easily wounded by criticism or insult. But those who have been devalued by society are unusually sensitive to the signals they receive from the dominant culture. . . . Listen to what those in need are saying and . . . also to what is not being said.[4]

Lupton's words are now burned into my heart.

So, can God trust you to be his hands and feet to the least in your community? Our heavenly Father has not called us to look past someone's sin or to excuse it in any way. We are to always be aware of our own sinful nature and to be willing vessels of Christ's redemptive grace as we humbly recall our own redemptive stories. He may call on you to take a man or woman by the hand and help him or her discover the power of his Spirit to sin no more. The greatest soul winners I know are those who have not forgotten their life before salvation.

Stop and pray now that God will expose anything in your heart, soul, and mind that is tainted by pride, arrogance, or judgment toward anyone who bears the image of God.

5

Digging Deeper
to Bring Healing

When Jesus landed and saw a large crowd,
he had compassion on them and healed their sick.
MATTHEW 14:14, NIV (EMPHASIS ADDED)

IF WE'RE NOT CAREFUL, we can become program driven in our approach to reaching people with the gospel. Programs are fine, but often they are not designed to probe deeply into people's lives to get to the core of their issues, pain, and struggles—whatever it is they need to surrender to Christ. We must address the real barriers that block the flow of God's Spirit from penetrating their hearts.

In 2019, I had to have quadruple cardiac bypass surgery. During the weeks prior to diagnosis, I was feeling sluggish and tired and experiencing labored breathing. I couldn't walk very far without becoming exhausted, and climbing stairs became a chore. I went to the doctor almost daily trying to figure out what was wrong. Each time they checked my heart, and each time the EKG did not record any distress. So they sent me home without any further investigation or analysis.

Regardless of the doctors' opinions or what the readouts revealed, I knew something was wrong. So I continued to seek advice from various doctors until a heaven-sent nurse practitioner at our local hospital's emergency room convinced her supervisors to order a nuclear stress test with a contrast CAT scan instead of an EKG. The test revealed several blockages that should have given me a massive heart attack or stroke long ago. However, by God's grace, the test also revealed that I have a gene that creates natural bypasses, called collaterals, that form new blood vessels around each blockage. These collaterals provided my heart with an adequate blood supply, which caused the earlier EKGs to look normal. I was at death's door and didn't know it.

I thank God every day for that nurse who took a deeper look at my situation. She went beyond the customary and routine service of care to treat my issue. She ordered the exam I needed and went the second mile. She even put her own job at risk by arranging the test and finding a doctor who would sign off on the procedure when others refused. Her commitment to my health literally saved my life.

The first night I spent in my hospital room, I had a cardiac episode. I was told by the staff that if I had been at home and not surrounded by the best of medical care, I would have died. Without this nurse's devotion to my personal well-being, my life and ministry would have ended, or I could have suffered a debilitating outcome.

The nurse's care reminded me of how Jesus saw the crowd and instinctively knew they needed healing. When Jesus fed the five thousand, he did more than just preach a sermon series and serve a potluck meal of fish and bread. No, he spent time diagnosing and treating the deep and life-threatening illnesses of the sick. He touched their pain, relieved their suffering, and healed them.

When we are addressing someone's need, each of us must ask the question, Have I done enough? Are we penetrating the root condition in a person's life by just giving them food from our church pantry without exploring the deep-seated affliction that haunts them? When our churches host a block party or provide benevolent support, we must ask ourselves if there is more we could and should do.

Christ exceeded the routine standard care of ministry that we sometimes offer. He probed and asked questions that went beyond the surface. He listened to people's stories, connected to their grief, and discerned that a deeper degree of healing was required for many of them. Not unlike my nurse, Jesus would not turn away hurting men and women until he exposed the root of their distress and restored them to health spiritually and otherwise.

Christ's conscientious care for the wounded should oblige us to have the same level of concern for those we encounter in our daily walk. Whether at work, at church, in the community, or in our own homes, the Spirit of God compels us to bring his healing, wholeness, and balance to whomever we meet.

People are experts in hiding their pain. Many in the church hide their pain for years before they feel safe enough to bring it into the light. Our job is to provide an environment where they will feel secure enough to share their hurts and not cover them up with Christian jargon and proper church etiquette. We must find ways to dig deeper and to be a church that is committed to modeling honesty and being a safe place for people to shed years of suffering.

Most congregations want to provide care for church members and community members in crisis. However, many churches don't have the processes or training in place to assist the dozens or hundreds of people who may require their services. Severe damage can be done if recipients of care are mishandled by well-meaning but inexperienced or unqualified caregivers. Prudent pastors and church leaders will ensure that staff and volunteers have the proper training necessary to give the best care possible within the parameters of spiritual and pastoral care and leave the critical trauma care to qualified professionals.

My aim in writing this book is to make sure you have the basic elements in your life and church so that you can be used by God to bring more and more people to Christ. That won't happen if you aren't willing to love people where they are and if your church doesn't provide a safe place for people to be transparent and expose their struggles.

We can read all the books on evangelism, purchase all the kits to effectively share the gospel, and attend every conference that teaches us the latest and greatest tactics of outreach. But if there is no love in our hearts, hurting people will sense it from miles away, and they will never open their lives to us. We will only know people on the surface and never get a chance to go deeper, where true breakthrough and life change occur.

People followed Jesus because they knew he cared. And somehow he created safe spaces where he could touch the deep-seated issues that held them back and held them bound.

In *Organic Outreach for Churches*, Kevin Harney maintains that we must infuse evangelistic passion into our churches. Even raising the temperature by one degree will change everything, he says.

Harney describes a ministry as having a high outreach temperature "when its leaders and workers are consistently seeing nonchurched visitors attend and when these spiritual seekers are hearing about the amazing love of God, are having meaningful spiritual conversations, and are entering a relationship with Jesus."[5]

The main goal of a high-outreach church is to help people establish a growing relationship with Jesus. The goal is not to get them to join the church, visit the food pantry, enroll in a class, or place their children in the church's daycare. These things may contribute to achieving the goal, but they are not the objective.

The text says Jesus had compassion for the people. Then his concern led him to do more than preach to them. He did more than listen to their stories of pain—he healed them. He went deeper until the root cause of their distress was uncovered. We can't stop ministering to people until they are healed in body, soul, and spirit. But always remember that God has not called us to merely do good. We are called to bring forth the gospel. Whatever you do, make sure that Christ remains at the center.

The churches that thrive in the next ten years will be those that dig deeper into the lives of hurting people. They will provide or have access to ministry tools that seek to heal. Discipleship courses that address broken family dynamics, counseling services offered by trained professionals and laypeople, mentorship programs for youth and adults, and recovery, grief, and anxiety support systems for all ages will be basic requirements to dig deeper into the emotional trauma that permeates our communities today.

There is every indication that the next few years will require more from the caregiving sectors of our society. The pandemic left a generation of young people behind educationally, political and racial divisions are escalating, and families are becoming more fractured and broken. The body of Christ cannot sit on the sidelines and watch as our world crumbles. Yes, we will continue to pray and we will proclaim God's Word faithfully. But this tidal wave of pain in our world requires us to dig deeper and be the second-mile saints that Christ calls us to be (Matthew 5:41).

Is your church preparing for the tsunami wave of hurting humanity coming our way?

What are you doing to prepare yourself and your church to receive them? Are there other churches and ministry organizations you can learn from, books you can read, or conferences you can attend to become better equipped?

One way to discern what God may want your church to do in the community is to assess the members of your church. What skills, expertise, passions, and education does your congregation have that could contribute to a ministry in your community?

Dan Reiland Interview

Dan Reiland has been a pastor and leader for more than forty years. He worked closely with John C. Maxwell as executive pastor of Skyline Wesleyan Church in San Diego, and for the past twenty years he has served as executive director of leadership expansion at 12Stone Church in Lawrenceville, Georgia. He has invested in thousands of church leaders through church consulting, executive coaching, and his books Confident Leader!, Amplified Leadership, Leadership Alone Isn't Enough, *and* Shoulder to Shoulder.

Tyrone Barnette

What are the most pressing needs of people and the world today?

Dan Reiland

Anxiety is the number one thing people tell us when they come forward. There is an inner turmoil, a low-grade lack of peace that just doesn't go away.

We all need a deeper connection with truth and purpose that brings the inner peace that is missing. Lack of peace is dominating people's behavior and it's in our churches and communities.

Tyrone Barnette

What experiences are hindering churches today from reaching the community?

Dan Reiland

There is so much division and cultural unrest. So much misunderstanding. So much "cancel this" and "cancel that" going on.

We must create space for people to have conversations, space for people to listen to each other. That's what is broken.

When first-time visitors and guests come in, there is often as much hesitation or mistrust as there is hope. When we do get the opportunity to have a conversation, the important question is, Are you interested in a conversation or a debate?

A debate by nature has a winner and a loser. Somebody must win and someone has to lose. A debate declares someone is right and someone is wrong. We need to move toward a conversation. And whatever the church can do to create and foster conversation, we need to do that.

Tyrone Barnette

Jesus had compassion for people, and he spent time with them. Before he fed the five thousand, he heard them, he healed them. He spent time with them before feeding them. I'm not sure if we do that well today.

Dan Reiland

It's true that everyone is very busy. Everyone is in a hurry. What we need right now is to slow down. That's hard to do when you don't have time. Rather than driving our church agenda, we must first get on another's agenda. We must be able to get in their space to hear them. Things are so difficult because we are too busy to hear each other.

It's not that we back away from speaking the truth. It's just that we must lead with the heart, open the doors, and start the conversations. In my forty years of ministry, there has never been a larger gap between the perspective of the evangelical church and the perspective of the culture in general. The size of the gap requires more time to engage in conversation.

Tyrone Barnette

In your book *Leadership Alone Isn't Enough*, you have a chapter titled "Accept Your Divine Assignment."[6] When partnering with God, what is the pastor's and leader's responsibility?

Dan Reiland

Ephesians 4:11-13 makes it clear that the pastor carries the responsibility to equip leaders and the larger body of Christ for works of service. The pastor's job is to engage people in meaningful ministry in order to activate the serving heart of Christ within them. The pastors and the staff are mobilizers. We are to inspire, encourage, train, and mobilize the congregation to do the ministry.

We are called to mobilize the church to go out into the community. The purpose of the church continues after the worship service ends. It works best and goes further when everyone is aligned with the same vision.

Tyrone Barnette

You're the executive pastor of a very large church, and you've got a great staff. How do you motivate the congregation to be evangelistic and have an outreach focus when they see a professional staff that does it so wonderfully?

Dan Reiland

We tell stories all the time. I think consistently telling stories of life change, and making it possible for the congregation to hear the stories and see people get baptized makes them want to evangelize in their own lives. I think there is something supernatural in a baptism, and when non-Christians witness a baptism, they know something special just happened.

Tyrone Barnette

How should churches be thinking about building design in the future to really reach our community?

Dan Reiland

I think there's a trend for a smaller church building. There's a lot in play that verifies and affirms that. The megachurches with worship space for two thousand or more, led by pastors from the boomer generation face issues of succession because of the shortage of leaders who can or want to fill those pulpits once they retire. Even if God would fill those spots, I'm not sure the culture wants those big rooms right now.

I thank God for the seeker services with the hazers and lights and the creative elements that drew people in that way in the past. But the financial ramifications of the maintenance that's required in these very large buildings is calling for smaller spaces.

My good friend Nathan Artt is the founder and CEO of Ministry Solutions. He tells me they are building multiuse spaces, so that through the week there are things like childcare facilities, coffee shops, and business-oriented options for greater usage, and to help people in the community come and find jobs.

There's a church in New England that has "adopted" the majority of a city block and is now running a coffee shop, an auto repair facility to get your oil changed, and other cool ways to approach and move into the community—including, of course, a small space for a church. I love what they are doing!

I want us to be as creative as possible so we can engage life where people live. Don't automatically go out and start a Christian softball league. Go out and join the softball leagues already in the community and bring Christian faith to them.

Tyrone Barnette

What concerns do you have about the future? And what is your greatest hope?

Dan Reiland

My greatest concern is our lack of ability to talk to each other inside and outside the church. When we can't talk, or won't talk, or we just get frustrated, maybe angry, and stop talking, I think that makes solving things very complicated.

But I have great hope. I truly believe that the church, led by Christ, is the hope of the world. I truly believe the church is the light in a troubled world and in a dark time. Let's just keep talking and good leaders will find good solutions.

Tyrone Barnette

If readers want to contact you, how would they connect?

Dan Reiland

They can join The Pastor's Coach blog at danreiland.com.

6

How to Double Your Evangelism Ministry

He welcomed them and taught them about the Kingdom
of God, and he healed those who were sick.

LUKE 9:11

DO YOU AND YOUR CHURCH LONG to see people healed? Without a doubt we all desire to ensure that people receive Christ's spiritual healing. Our churches were built to provide places where the Word of God is preached and people can find the spiritual fulfillment that comes from a loving relationship with Christ and his church.

I would argue that spiritual healing is the most important domain in a person's life. Out of the spiritual sphere, the whole of a person's life can be touched and transformed. To ignore spiritual healing is to inhibit God's power from bringing order to chaotic lives. No amount of human effort or wisdom can compare to the supremacy of God's Spirit to bring all-inclusive change and transformation to the human condition.

Yet a Christian or church should not stop with providing spiritual healing alone. Jesus touched and rehabilitated more than the spiritual aspects of people's lives. He ministered to the whole individual. He reached and altered their emotional, relational, economic, and physical needs. Christ did not stop short of identifying and removing buried obstacles that clogged the arteries of the human heart from experiencing the fullness of the abundant life he offered.

This is the assignment of every church. Church leaders must create a ministry model to provide comprehensive and complete care for their community and congregation by extending healing for the total person or family. Our job is to be attuned to what is out of rhythm in a person's life, and not to merely diagnose it or identify it, but to solve and renew whatever is broken and out of alignment with the life-giving power and Spirit of Christ.

A brief word of caution is appropriate here concerning counseling and doing the difficult work of therapy without the proper training. The church is an excellent place to form deep and meaningful relationships where real life change occurs as people share their lives with one another. However, some people require more specialized care than the average church can provide to deal with their psychological and mental trauma. At our church, we make it clear that we provide spiritual and pastoral care, using the Bible as our guide. When we discern there is an issue that is beyond the scope of our expertise, we have a list of certified Christian counselors and therapists to whom we can refer people.

My wife and I adopted our eldest son when he was six years old. During his senior year of high school he developed mental and behavioral issues that were later diagnosed as schizophrenia. Our church family prayed for us and did everything they could to aid our family through the next few years of difficulty. We knew we needed to engage professionals to give our son the care he needed. Our willingness to be transparent and vulnerable with our story gave others in our church and community permission to reveal their struggles with mental illness. We discovered there were dozens of families suffering in silence because of the stigma that often surrounds mental illness. Digging deeper may require the church to allow mental health professionals or a qualified parachurch organization to support their work.

Likewise, the church can develop a pastoral care or congregational care ministry that addresses many of the emotional and mental health needs of the church and community. There are many online programs, small-group-based curriculums, and local colleges and seminaries that offer training to equip your leadership.

I rejoice that many churches are now learning to address with prayer, preaching, and partnership the psychological, economic, and educational maladies pervasive in our society.

It takes an unselfish church and Christians with hearts of compassion to perceive and comprehend societal and personal pain that tunnels beneath the surface, hidden from view. God desires to give the church the spiritual gifts of wisdom, discernment, and mercy to address all aspects of human need.

This commitment comes with a high price tag. It requires a spirit of self-sacrifice and an enormous personal investment in the lives of others. God often calls us to minister to a population of people who may not hold our values or have our life experiences. But like Jesus, we are called to bring healing to each one and not turn any away.

How do we do this? First, we must be willing for God to use us as his vessels to provide care. Be forewarned that everyone you try to help may not be ready to receive it. Attempting to motivate someone to change or accept assistance is a major barrier to cross. Our job is not to force care on someone, but to project a willingness and openness to maintain a posture of availability while trusting the Holy Spirit to open doors of opportunity. Few people want to be told what to do or hear a barrage of "shoulds and should nots." Our job is not to add stress to people's lives but to demonstrate how Christ can bring balance and serenity if they are receptive. Even Jesus asked the man at the pool of Bethesda, "Would you like to get well?" (John 5:6). Sadly, many will reject our offer of support, but we serve nevertheless.

Our motivation and obligation are centered on the mission that is born out of pure love for Christ and the people we serve. Jesus' faithfulness to the people was tied to his compassion for them. It is hard to be devoted to people we have no compassion for. Therefore, we must ask God to search our hearts and soften the areas we have hardened against others.

Our world is so divided today. Let's use this time of societal, political, and religious division to stand out as a people of compassion, especially making an effort to engage with those who don't look like us, act like us, or believe like us. These darkened and divided times are just the right atmosphere for the light of Christ to shine through us brighter than ever.

Second, we must make a commitment to do whatever it takes to facilitate healing. Every church I know confesses a responsibility to reach its community. There is a high value on outreach that distinguishes the church. Usually there are words to that effect in the vision or mission statement or displayed on the walls.

"We are committed to the Great Commission."

"Souls are our top focus."

"Outreach is one of our top priorities because it is how we show love to our community."

I've read declarations like those in dozens of churches. But most would agree that these platitudes are more aspirational and motivational than lived out in the life of the church as a whole or by its individual members.

It is difficult to get the average church member to join the evangelism team. People are generally apprehensive about sharing their faith, particularly in the programmed, organized way that many church-sponsored evangelism initiatives are organized.

Could we attract more people to join our teams if we began promoting our evangelism and outreach ministries in terms of providing healing to those who are broken rather than an intimidating neighborhood door-knocking activity? Don't get me wrong, we must share our faith and invite our community to accept Christ. But I have discovered that many more Christians participate in evangelistic movements when I frame the ministry in words that advocate healing brokenness in people's lives.

People joined in droves when we invited them to participate in a ministry initiative that brings healing to families experiencing the effects of Alzheimer's disease. It is easier to get people involved with our grief ministry and ask them to care for those who have undergone a loss through death, job loss, financial setback, or prolonged sickness than to get them to join the evangelism team. Dozens connect with our ministry through several area nursing homes but would never have taken part in an evangelism drive.

In each of these ministries, and several more, everything an evangelism ministry would do is being done. We simply don't call it evangelism; we refer to it as "healing brokenness." We center the ministry on Jesus with a clear presentation of the gospel, but the people who volunteer don't necessarily join with the goal of doing evangelism. However, when they see how easy it is to share their faith, they are hooked. They have a hand in bringing someone to Christ and discover the rewards of living an evangelistic life.

When I was growing up, my mother knew how to get me to eat vegetables by placing them in other dishes I liked. She made zucchini spaghetti years before it became a popular alternative to pasta. How can you redesign your evangelism ministry to make it less intimidating to your congregation and more integrated with other church programs?

What mental health professionals or agencies in your community can your church partner with? What resources can you find to train your staff and volunteers to provide spiritual and pastoral care?

7

Do You Love the World?

He had compassion on them because they were like sheep
without a shepherd. So he began teaching them many things.
MARK 6:34

DO YOU LOVE THE WORLD? I'm not talking about loving *worldly*
things, but loving the people outside your four walls.

It's a sobering question. Most of us would say *yes*. But do you
love the world as Jesus does? How about as God does in John 3:16?

I must challenge you to think about this at a subterranean
level. Ask yourself these questions and explore them in that place
where your secret prejudices live. Give the Spirit of God permission to search your soul and unearth irritations and biases you
harbor toward certain people or groups. If you are honest, you
will uncover thoughts, judgments, and opinions that you need
to repent of, secret hostilities and aggressions in the darkness of
your soul toward people you may never have even met but only
experienced through the perceptions of others.

It is in this very spot that God's Spirit wants to work on you.

It's where he wants to teach you to love at a level you never thought possible. Most people rarely stay in this corner of their soul long enough to be truly transformed. It's too uncomfortable to be reminded of how far we are from Christ's example. But I encourage you to linger here a little longer because this is where real ministry fulfillment can be found.

But if you're tempted to remain in your bubble of friends and family, consider these words from Jesus:

> If you love those who love you, what credit is that to you? Even sinners love those who love them. And if you do good to those who are good to you, what credit is that to you? Even sinners do that. And if you lend to those from whom you expect repayment, what credit is that to you? Even sinners lend to sinners, expecting to be repaid in full. But love your enemies, do good to them, and lend to them without expecting to get anything back. Then your reward will be great, and you will be children of the Most High, because he is kind to the ungrateful and wicked. Be merciful, just as your Father is merciful.[7]

Years ago, these words of Jesus radically changed my life. I prided myself on being an impartial guy who loved everyone. I boasted inwardly that I could get along with anyone. But all that was challenged when God called me to embrace a group of people whose lifestyle choices I found repugnant. The specifics are not important—allow God to speak to you about your own prejudices and attitudes—but my heart was hard and all I could see were our differences.

Through a close friend, I met a man who wanted to know more about Jesus. He trusted me to help him grapple with some of his questions and concerns about Christianity. I agreed to help, but only reluctantly, with an attitude that was far from Christlike. I gave short answers and treated the man with little warmth and limited compassion. Somehow, he wasn't put off by my unenthusiastic demeanor and wanted to set up additional times to talk.

Despite my reprehensible behavior, this man drew closer to Christ and found a renewed relationship with him that resulted in a complete change in his lifestyle and choices. But even as I watched God change this man's heart, my own heart remained like a stone. I still held the same prejudices and judgmental attitudes.

Eventually, this man had enough of my foul spirit and pulled away from me. I'm grateful that he never turned away from Jesus. He remained a committed believer until his death—which came only a year later. I still carry deep regrets for my actions and my attitudes, and I am in awe of God's ability to use broken people like me in spite of ourselves.

Through a series of events, God arrested my heart. He showed me how I had been willfully acting in sin toward one of his children. It was the first time I could recall sensing that God was ashamed of me for the way I behaved. I have long since repented, and over the years God has shown me other areas that needed renovation in my soul toward those he loves. It seems that each year God pulls away another layer of prejudice from my heart, like peeling an onion.

Jay Pathak and Dave Runyon wrote a book called *The Art of Neighboring*. It is one of my favorite books that reminds me to love. I underlined and starred this section:

Jesus never called us to use a bait-and-switch approach, where we become friends with people *only* to share spiritual truths with them. We are called to love people—period. Whether those people ever take any steps toward God is beside the point. We are called to love our neighbors unconditionally, without expecting anything in return. The Great Commandment says, "Love your neighbor as yourself." The commandment ends there, with no other expectations given. Thus good neighboring is an end in itself.[8]

That encounter was over thirty years ago, and since that time I have been tutored by God's Spirit in learning to love this world as Christ does. Loving people and having compassion for them does not mean I embrace someone's lifestyle or agree with their choices. My love for those I disagree with does not require me to abandon my beliefs, but rather it is my beliefs and convictions that compel me to love.

I discovered that we cannot do effective evangelism and outreach without having a genuine and authentic love for the world. Like my friend, people know when we don't care for them. They can see through our fake expressions of tolerance. But Christ has not called us to simply be tolerant of the world. He has called us to love the people of the world as he does.

It is a privilege that God trusts us with other people's pain. Many are already broken and bruised when they come to us for help. I imagine that God looks for compassionate Christians to whom he can direct these people for help—someone who will be tender and patient, who will walk sympathetically with wounded people as they seek restoration. When truth must be shared, they will not deliver it with the blunt end of a hammer—with harsh words that worsen the already exposed wound. Instead, they will regard the opportunity to care as a sacred trust from God and the person's heart as a sacred space where the Spirit's power can initiate transformation.

It is true, Christ calls us to not love the world or the things in the world (1 John 2:15). But in this instance, he is calling us not to be in love with *the world system*. The world system includes its politics, ideals, standards, morals, and ethics. We are not to conform to the sinful aspects of the world's system but to love the people of the world who need to see Christ through us and sense his love from us.

Many non-Christians will not accept Christ as their Savior because they've had a negative experience with one of Christ's children. They have been turned off by the actions and attitudes of God's people who have placed politics, ethnicity, social class, and other affiliations above our relationship with Christ. And until we place Christ first, we will continue to do harm unintentionally and intentionally, and many will reject him. Sadly, their blood will be on our hands.

Christ's church is made up of every flavor of humanity and is stocked with the good, the bad, and the ugly. The church is filled with broken people who mount pulpits, sing in choirs, answer phones, and serve at every level of ministry. As damaged and defective as we are, we are still Christ's first-round picks to change the world. Thank God that, by his grace, he uses us despite our flaws. Somehow his piercing light shines through us and transforms both sinner and saint who yield to his Spirit.

On that day when fish and bread were served, another meal was also passed around. The "fruit salad" of the Holy Spirit (Galatians 5:22-23) was distributed to everyone present. Jesus and his disciples served up a nourishing portion of love, joy, peace, patience, kindness, goodness, faithfulness, gentleness, and self-control. The people left satisfied, not just from *what* was served (fish and bread), but because of the *spirit* in which it was served.

Several times a month, I sit at one of my favorite restaurants for a meal. The food is not the best I've ever had. But I go for the gracious and welcoming spirit of the wait and kitchen staff. I sense their care for me, and they demonstrate that I matter to them. This should be a characteristic that is pervasive in our churches. The saying is true: People don't care how much we know until they know how much we care. Let's serve up the fruit of the Spirit and watch people come back again and again for more.

Do you love the world as God does? If not, why not? Until we do, he may not be able to trust us with it.

8

Evening Is Approaching, and There's No Time to Waste

*As evening approached, the disciples came to him and said,
"This is a remote place, and it's already getting late. Send the crowds away,
so they can go to the villages and buy themselves some food."*
MATTHEW 14:15, NIV (EMPHASIS ADDED)

EVENING WAS APPROACHING and soon the night sky would be filled with stars. The people were far from their homes and faced a long walk back. In the disciples' minds they had done enough work for one day. Enough preaching, teaching, serving, and listening to the demands of the crowd. The presence of the shifting shadows of dusk confirmed that they had done enough. "Let's pack it up and go home" was their refrain. "We've done enough."

The attitude of the disciples typifies the position of many Christians in the twenty-first century: "We've done enough." We focus on how much time we have given and how long we have labored instead of how little time remains for those who have not yet embraced Christ. We need a fervent sense of urgency to meet the needs of others. As Christians, we often display little interest in making every moment count to bring others closer to Christ's Kingdom. Remember, evening is approaching.

Many of us have experienced regret when we learned that a family member or friend unexpectedly passed away before we had time to return their call or reach out in some way. We intended to phone them, send out an email or text, or stop by just to say hi. When the Holy Spirit has brought a loved one to our mind and we failed to act on the prompting in a timely manner, we may have found out later that they had experienced a major crisis and our procrastination caused us to miss an opportunity to be there for them. It is on these occasions that we become keenly aware of the diminishing sands of time.

It has been more than two thousand years since Jesus ascended into heaven. In Acts 1:8, he invites his disciples to "be my witnesses, telling people about me everywhere." Days after the Ascension, God's Spirit would empower the disciples, and from that moment on, they steadfastly proclaimed the gospel message to everyone because they believed Christ would come back at any moment. They wanted to deliver souls to him on his arrival. They recalled his parables about being ready when the master or bridegroom returns. No one wanted to be the unprofitable servant described in Matthew 25, who buried his talent while others gained an increase. None wanted to be like the foolish virgins who didn't bring enough oil to the vigil and missed the bridegroom.

I wonder, do we today have that same sense of urgency and expectation of the Lord's return? Do we see that the evening is closer and that it is getting late in the day?

I want to live in the constant knowledge that Jesus may return at any moment. I do not want to be caught with my work undone. I especially do not want to maintain a lackadaisical attitude toward evangelism and assume that I have far more time than I actually do to win souls for Christ.

How do we inspire the contemporary church to take seriously the need to be "about [our] Father's business" as Jesus was?[9] What is the Father's business? Do we know? Jesus' business was to seek and save those who were lost (Luke 19:10).

This world is rapidly moving away from the principles and practices that reflect God's vision for a redemptive community. Paul warns us in 2 Timothy 4:1-5 (NIV):

> In the presence of God and of Christ Jesus, who will judge the living and the dead, and in view of his appearing and his kingdom, I give you this charge: Preach the word; be prepared in season and out of season; correct, rebuke and encourage—with great patience and careful instruction. For the time will come when people will not put up with sound doctrine. Instead, to suit their own desires, they will gather around them a great number of teachers to say what their itching ears want to hear. They will turn their ears away from the truth and turn aside to myths. But you, keep your head in all situations, endure hardship, do the work of an evangelist, discharge all the duties of your ministry.

Paul's warning about the future state of our world should distress our hearts, but it should also activate our faith and create an evangelistic fervor. God is calling us to reach the world for him. It is truly late in the evening and time until Christ's return is shorter now than ever before. We must not waste one more moment or squander one more year allowing Satan to distract us from our Great Commission mandate with trivial pursuits that champion nationalism, racism, sexism, classism, or any other man-made isms.

Evening is approaching! Let's not face it alone.

Is your church an evangelistically focused congregation?

Ask your leaders and members which of these probing statements apply to them:

a. I have invited an unchurched friend or family member to church in the past six months.

b. I support the church committing at least 10 percent of the annual budget to reach new people through outreach events.

c. I have introduced myself in church to a new member or guest in the past month.

d. I have prayed for a specific unchurched person over the past month.

e. I would be willing to ask an unchurched person to my home for dinner once every six months.

f. I have participated in an outreach event in my church over the past six months.

g. The primary purpose of our church is to carry out the Great Commission.

h. I would support the pastor spending more time after church greeting nonmembers than members.

i. I have shared my faith with at least one person over the past month.

j. I would join a new group or help pioneer a new church that wants to reach new people.

Fred Luter Interview

Pastor Fred Luter is the senior pastor of Franklin Avenue Baptist Church in New Orleans, Louisiana, where he has faithfully served since 1986. The church has grown tremendously under his leadership, and he has established several community-based ministries in New Orleans and beyond. In 2012, he was unanimously elected as the first African American president of the Southern Baptist Convention. He is a frequent conference speaker and sought-after mentor.

Tyrone Barnette

Your church went through a rebuilding period after Hurricane Katrina devastated New Orleans and the Gulf Coast in 2005. You also had experience during the pandemic when again your church was dispersed. What are some of the things that worked for you?

Fred Luter

It's a great question because our folks were spread out everywhere after Katrina hit. But one of the key things that helped us to gather people was having access to the Internet. Eighty percent of our city was underwater, and our church had nine feet of water in it, so we could not worship there. Having access to the Internet allowed me to connect to our members spread across the country. It kept the line of communication open until we were ready to receive people back in the city of New Orleans and start having services again.

The key was keeping in touch with our members through social media, other media, and our website. That really helped us connect with people to get them back home. Just like every church had to do in the pandemic when we couldn't meet, we had to learn to embrace technology to keep us connected.

Today, we can't resist technology and social media to minister to our congregation and to reach the community. Every church, regardless of its size, has an opportunity to have a worldwide ministry with the Internet. They just need to use it. With the Internet, our community is global, not just local.

Tyrone Barnette

Your church is a fairly large congregation and blessed with a great staff. How do you keep the people in the church connected to evangelism and outreach when they may think they pay you and the staff to do all that for them? How do you get the whole church involved in personal evangelism in their daily lives?

Fred Luter

First, you have to just challenge them and make them realize that evangelism is for everybody. Yes, we do have people on staff who are kind of experts in that field. But every member is an evangelist.

So we challenge people. I've challenged people for years at Franklin Avenue with a concept called FRANgelism, meaning that everybody in the church has an unsaved or unchurched Friend, Relative, Associate (coworker), Neighbor. I tell my church that they have a responsibility as believers to share their testimonies by sharing what God has done for them.

We try to break it down into three areas: your life before you got saved, how you got saved, and then your life after salvation. They share that with those lost individuals and then invite them to our local church. So before they may ever hear me preach or the choir sing, they have heard the gospel and may even have surrendered to Christ.

Do all of them do it? Nope, they don't. But a lot of them do understand the fact that evangelism is for every born-again believer.

Tyrone Barnette

What do you see as the greatest hindrances the church faces today when attempting to reach our community? And why does it feel like it's harder to do evangelism today than it has been in years past?

Fred Luter

You know, I think the greatest hindrance to reaching out to people is that people just get complacent. They get to the point of thinking, *I got mine, I'm okay. Let the world get theirs.* That's the wrong attitude to have. So pastors from the pulpit and leaders in Sunday school classes and throughout the church have got to challenge people not to be at ease and to feel the urgency of evangelism. We have to keep inviting new people to our churches, because we don't want to get to the point where the church becomes like a club where everybody knows each other but we are not touching new people and discipling them. So I think the greatest hindrance is people getting complacent and feeling that they don't need to reach out to new people in their community.

Tyrone Barnette

What do you think the needs are of the people we're trying to reach? What are they crying out for that we can provide?

Fred Luter

They're crying out for people who are authentic. They need to see people who are real about their faith. And that's why developing relationships is so important. We have to develop relationships with people in our neighborhoods and communities, with coworkers and in our jobs, and on college campuses. We need to let them see our light. People are living in a dark world, and believers need to be lights and salt in society.

People are looking for things that are real, and we're living in a day and time where people can't tell who's real and who's not.

When you and I grew up, we didn't have a choice about coming to church. My mom made me go to church every week. I tell folks that she gave me my first drug problem. She drug me to church and Bible study all the time, and that's not happening today. People are not coming to church like they used to. So we have to go to them.

We especially have to go back to teaching parents how to be parents because real change starts in the home. Learning values starts in the home. I'm burdened by the lack of parenting in the home. That's a major problem I see. Where are the parents when our youth are out in the street at two o'clock in the morning? We are missing training in the home, and the church needs to focus there. It's not the government's or the school's responsibility to teach what the home should be giving, and the church can help with that.

My greatest hope is when I see young families coming to church. I realize we're not reaching everybody, but we are reaching some, and that gives me hope. But it starts in the home, and this is where the church can make a difference.

9

No More Excuses

*Late in the afternoon the twelve disciples came to him and said, "Send the
crowds away to the nearby villages and farms, so they can find food and
lodging for the night. There is nothing to eat here in this remote place."*

But Jesus said, "You feed them."

*"But we have only five loaves of bread and two fish," they answered. "Or
are you expecting us to go and buy enough food for this whole crowd?"*

LUKE 9:12-13

"THERE ARE THREE THINGS IN LIFE that are certain: death, taxes,
and excuses."

I will never forget the time one of my high school teachers
called me out for my excuses when I didn't want to do something
that was expected of me. Back then, I had no idea the impact his
words would continue to have in my life as I have become a leader.

As Christians, we are too often full of excuses for why we are
not carrying out our Master's mandate by fulfilling the Great
Commission.

There are legitimate reasons that could be used as justification
by some Christians and churches for not moving forward with
evangelistic fervor. Most are skilled at making excuses that seem
appropriate but fall short of exempting us from the responsibility
for the souls of our families, neighbors, and friends.

Here are a few common excuses made by Christians:

- "I don't have time."
- "I'm afraid I may not know a Scripture or have an answer for something I'm asked."
- "I've not been trained."
- "Evangelism is the pastor's job."
- "I don't know any nonbelievers or unchurched folks."

The list can go on and on. However, most of them start with what an individual can't do. They do not take into account what the Lord can and will do if we simply yield ourselves to him. Each of these excuses reveals a lack of faith and dependency on the Lord. Excuses are normally focused on our own inadequacies rather than our sufficiency in the Lord and his abundant supply.

In the text, the disciples came to Jesus to encourage him to close down this evangelistic event because of the lateness of the hour and the geographical restraints of the gathering. They brought rational excuses for Jesus to pronounce the benediction and let them all go home.

Notice that no one offered a solution to keep the affair alive or a suggestion on how to bend the challenges to their advantage. They only saw the problem that produced excuses to quit instead of shifting their thinking to move in a unique and innovative way and continue the revival. Nowhere is it recorded that any of the disciples celebrated the fact that so many of their countrymen had come together in one place to hear and experience the ministry of Jesus. They saw the problem and not the potential.

It's easy to convince yourself that you've done enough and have taken an enterprise as far as you can. That's okay if the project or venture is something that has little impact on the organization, community, or Kingdom of God. But how do you quit when the outcome of your efforts can have an eternal impact on the lives of the people you serve? How does one pack it all up and move on when God has presented such a great opportunity to make a dramatic shift in people's lives?

There is great wisdom in knowing how and when to set an appropriate pace as you pursue your mission, so you don't hit a wall or experience burnout. Jesus knew when to take a break and he never allowed himself to be hurried, stressed, or pressured. But don't sit out too long.

On the hillside, God had delivered five thousand men, plus their wives and children, to Jesus and the disciples. With an estimated fifteen thousand people present, this is the largest assembly they will ever have the privilege to minister to. And they are willing to walk away from the greatest evangelistic event of their lives.

Rather than create solutions, they manufacture excuses not to advance. Making excuses is easier and provides us cover from criticism, but we squander the potential and possibilities for greater Kingdom impact when we don't move forward. And sadly, when we quit, we prevent unbelievers from being exposed to ministry that could have played a part in their spiritual journey with Christ.

Early in our ministry, we faced all types of obstacles that could have set us back or made us give up and close down our ministry operation. There were a few seasons when it made sense to stop, retreat, or simply pack it up and resign. Corporately and personally, I have been at this crossroads.

There have been times when governmental regulations hindered us from building and expanding our ministry. Dozens of times, we could have given up. However, with every obstacle we faced, the church board did not make excuses and somehow came up with inventive ways to keep moving. I'm grateful for their faithful persistence.

Over the years, we faced financial constraints, relationship strains within the church, persons who opposed the vision, and dozens of other challenges familiar to any church. With every obstacle and at every trial, we have been graced to keep our focus on the souls of the men, women, boys, and girls God has entrusted to our congregation's care. Primary to our sense of purpose and calling, we have kept the eternal destinies of the people we are called to influence for Christ at the forefront of our minds. It drives our programs, shapes our budget, and deploys our people throughout the metro Atlanta area to make a difference.

Each church is responsible for the community that surrounds it. The homes, apartments, businesses, and schools that are clustered around the physical church building are within the church's missional obligation. Whether the community is in a period of racial, economic, or social transition, it is my belief that the church must find a way to overcome any obstacle or impediment with some new strategy to make Jesus known.

What challenges do you face today that are tempting you to quit? Confess your frustration or fear to God and ask for his divine guidance and power to overcome it.

10

Share the Needs

As evening approached, the disciples came to him and said,
"This is a remote place, and it's already getting late. Send the crowds away,
so they can go to the villages and buy themselves some food."

Jesus replied, "They do not need to go away.
You give them something to eat."
MATTHEW 14:15-16, NIV

THE DISCIPLES' REQUEST to send the people away seems both logical and prudent. The disciples didn't have the resources to meet the enormous demand, and they assumed the people would be able to fend for themselves if they went to the nearest villages to buy their own food. But if Jesus had sent them away, we—and all the people—would have missed out on witnessing God's miraculous provision.

Members of our churches are giving a larger portion of their income to various nonprofits than to their own churches. Worthy causes such as the Red Cross, World Vision, the Salvation Army, local charities, hospitals, and international mission organizations receive far more than the average church. Much of that money comes from the pockets of church members. They transfer their revenue and participate in other ventures outside the church because the local church has not spent sufficient time cultivating and developing its members to serve their own church.

There is nothing wrong with giving to parachurch and mission-driven organizations, or to hospitals and colleges. We should support any cause that touches our hearts and reflects our values and aspirations. Nevertheless, we are to ensure that the primary place we invest our time, talent, and treasure is with our local congregation (Malachi 3:10).

I bring this up because if a member's local church demonstrates little evidence of really making a difference in the community or around the world, the member may not give as generously. If there is no vision or effort to reach beyond the four walls of the church, it may limit the church's capacity to raise funds or enlist volunteers to give of themselves for ministry.

It took me years to become comfortable asking the people in my church to give. I had seen church leaders manipulate people to give rather than motivate them to contribute to the mission of the church. I recall leaders using various gimmicks to persuade people to give a specific amount of money. I saw pastors take up two or three offerings in one service until they reached the amount they expected. When I became a pastor, I vowed not to operate our church with those tactics. I said as little as I could about giving, so as to avoid being associated with those methods.

My reluctance to talk about money, or to even share the legitimate financial needs of the church, hindered us in our early years. Because I rarely spoke of those needs, members assumed the church had all the resources required to function. The bills were paid, lights stayed on, the staff performed at a high level, and we were reaching our community. For a while I was content with this arrangement, until I saw dozens of our church members making tremendous financial commitments to other ministries or nonprofits.

After years of this, I finally asked a couple I had a close personal relationship with why they felt the need to give such a large gift to a particular organization. Their contribution was spotlighted in the local paper, and I wondered why they did not subsidize a similar project we were carrying out. They were generous tithers and served faithfully on various teams in our church.

Their answer changed my approach to ministry and influenced how I communicate about money and the needs of the church. They said they didn't know we needed it. They weren't aware of what our particular ministry did throughout the community, and it never crossed their minds that the church was already participating in an area they were passionate about.

Our church served the community but rarely informed the congregation of the tremendous life change produced throughout the week in our various programs. We got so busy serving the people and carrying out our ministry functions that we did not take time at the conclusion of some events to celebrate and share the successful testimony with the larger church. We just moved on to the next adventure and launched into a new initiative. Much of the congregation was not aware of our ministry impact outside of Sunday. Therefore, members didn't contribute.

Like the disciples, I was sending people away from our church to go and participate somewhere else. We had no mechanism to educate our people on how they could get involved in our church beyond the typical Sunday programming. And similarly, we weren't staying connected to donors who were joining our outreach efforts financially and personally. So we'd get a lot of one-time gifts but not many recurring gifts to support the effort continually.

To remedy this oversight, we now host an annual event called the Global Impact Celebration. It is an entire weekend that highlights the church's outreach mission. We invite everyone in the church to a Friday night rally and have all our ministries' trusted partners present. There is food, testimonies from people whose lives have been changed, and various points of engagement for every age. From our youth to the senior adults, everyone participates for the entire weekend.

Saturday is a mission outreach day. We blitz the community with all types of service projects or carry out one major function that all ages can join. New people sign up and get immersed in and exposed to the work of ministry.

Sunday is the culmination of the weekend with a powerful celebration. Our church family makes a financial pledge for the next year to support various mission causes we have highlighted over the weekend. Members make pledges to support our recovery program, an orphanage in Africa, a project providing clean water in Uganda, help for sex-trafficking survivors on the streets of Atlanta, projects to benefit the public schools in our area, or dozens of other projects that we champion.

Every church must educate its members on what the church does missionally. Don't assume that everyone knows. Find creative ways to illustrate how your church is fulfilling the Great Commission—and celebrate the success stories.

How do you keep your church connected to outreach? How do you recruit new people to get involved? What new ministry opportunities do you foresee for your church? In what ways do you honor and encourage your faithful volunteers?

11

Developing a Whatever-It-Takes Mindset

That evening the disciples came to him and said, "This is a
remote place, and it's already getting late. Send the crowds
away so they can go to the villages and buy food for themselves."
But Jesus said, "That isn't necessary—you feed them."

MATTHEW 14:15-16

IN 1993, I WAS GRACED BY GOD to plant Peace Baptist Church in
the Atlanta metro area. For thirty years, I have been blessed to serve
as the pastor of the most loving, giving, and surrendered people I
have ever known. We started out with a vision to reach our local
community and have seen thousands give themselves to Christ
as leaders sacrificially exhibited a whatever-it-takes approach to
ministry.

However, at times there has been a struggle to move into new
territory, launch new ideas, and advance the vision. At each season
of resistance, the church leaders weren't willing initially to pay the
price or give up their own comfort for the sake of ministry progress.

In Matthew 14:15, it was not the five thousand who were asking
to go home. The people were content being where they were and
absorbing more and more of Jesus' words of encouragement and

instruction. They had endured the long walk from their homes and were willing to skip dinner to feast on Jesus' message. A full belly was not more important to them than a satisfied soul. So they lingered, waiting to digest one more morsel of truth from the Master's lips.

In fact, it was the disciples who wanted to end the meeting and send the people away to feed themselves.

Dr. Bob Whitesel writes in *Growth by Accident, Death by Planning: How Not to Kill a Growing Congregation*, "When ministry stalls to a halt, it generally is not the masses that bring activity to a close. Regrettably, it tends to be the church's leadership who push the pause button and are eager to pull the plug."[10]

It is wise to shut down an enterprise if a ministry activity or focus has run its course. I would be the first to recommend that a particular ministry program is powered down and given a decent burial when it is no longer effective. Energy, resources, and attention could go to some other area of ministry that needs it much more and could benefit from an infusion of new life and assets. Likewise, a ministry may need to be suspended or cut if the leaders and volunteers are burned out, not properly prepared, or so frustrated that they can no longer contribute to its success.

Additionally, if the demands of a particular ministry program mean that a participant's family suffers in order to keep it alive, the program must be reworked. The families of staff, leaders, and volunteers must take priority over all ministry obligations and commitments.

Typically, the number one reason a ministry stalls or stops is credited to the church leadership's unenthusiastic and lackluster appetite to see it go forward. Resembling the disciples' attitude, ministry stops because the leaders initiate a stoppage, slowdown, or strike. The price tag of serving has exceeded the leaders' personal limits of self-sacrifice. They are no longer willing to come early to set up or stay late to break down. They are no longer enthusiastic about reaching new people and are consistently ill-prepared for the event. As a result, these burned-out and dispassionate leaders may sabotage the ministry in some way to give a reason to abandon ship and set sail for calmer waters and easier places to serve within the church. Many times a ministry activity has died because the leaders refused to feed it and give it the attention it required. In the end, it suffered a slow death of inaction and neglect.

How Do You Get a Church to Maintain a Whatever-It-Takes Mindset?

Serving is a primary theme throughout the Bible. Every church has to have within its DNA a core value of service that drives every aspect of the ministry. This is particularly important when reaching the community outside the church.

One of the most complimentary comments visitors can make about a church is that it's committed to serving others, especially the unchurched. How a church engages and deliberately extends itself to the community and those who are not members speaks volumes about the attitude and Christlike spirit of the church. This biblical norm must be modeled by the core leaders and chiefly present in the senior leader for the entire congregation to adopt it as an indispensable quality of their church.

As pastor, I have come to realize that much of what occurs in our church is more caught than taught. People watch and mimic behaviors they have witnessed and see lived out in real time by leadership. We all know it is better to see a sermon than to hear one, and self-denying servanthood communicates at a level much louder than any megaphone.

A self-sacrificing servant's heart is the first characteristic I look for in a person when I hire a paid staff member or when I look for someone to assume a volunteer leadership role. I know that at various points and in most seasons of ministry, they will be called upon to go well beyond the job description, assignment, or 5:00 p.m. quitting time. Without a whatever-it-takes mindset, they will put a lid on how far that ministry area will progress and what true Kingdom impact it could have.

Some churches that are growing and reaching their community hinder future growth because they don't want to add an additional service to accommodate the increase. One or more ministry areas may not be willing to make the personal sacrifice or adjustment to launch the new service.

A leader may think, *A second or third service would mean I must come to church earlier or leave later. I will have to raise more volunteers, and I don't want to work that hard.* Leaders may resist having to acquire additional skills or learn how to use new technology for the digital age. At each refusal to change and meet new challenges, such leaders place a lid on how far the ministry can expand.

Perhaps leaders are unwilling to embrace the new racial or socioeconomic status of people who have moved into the neighborhood. Attempting to reach new people would mean leaders have to stretch beyond a racial, cultural, or social barrier and confront their own prejudices and intolerances. To effectively reach a changing community, the staff and key volunteer leaders must develop a passion for the community.

To sustain an empathetic heart for the neighborhood, leaders can participate in some of the secular community events, work with the local public schools, attend local homeowners' meetings, conduct periodic surveys of the community, and ensure that a fair percentage of the church's leadership comes from the surrounding neighborhood. All these practices and more will bond the heart of the church to the community. The church will see its community as a vital part of its ministry, and the community will embrace the ministry and see the church as an essential and necessary part of the neighborhood.

This goodwill starts with the willingness of church leadership to adopt a whatever-it-takes mindset to be the church beyond its four walls.

Whenever there is an issue or some sort of conflict arising in the community, the church needs to figure out how to respond. Deploy volunteers to the local schools when there is a need because of low test scores or some other crisis where the church can offer support. When crime or a natural disaster strikes the community, develop creative solutions that can improve the situation so the community knows the church cares.

I read the local paper every day and watch the news to look for ways our church can respond to the tragedies that occur near us. A house fire, an unfortunate accidental death on the highway, or a business that is in trouble are reasons for us to arrange for our members to take some action to assist, if possible. We often offer our building for funerals to families who do not have a church home. We have adopted ten nursing homes in our area, providing monthly worship services in each facility and taking responsibility for each resident over the holidays by delivering gifts. From prison ministry to distributing a million pounds of food annually, it takes an army of dedicated and devoted members who possess a whatever-it-takes mindset to care for our neighbors.

How do you inspire your leaders to possess a whatever-it-takes mindset? What do you do to avoid ministry burnout and ensure leaders have a healthy balance between working in ministry and prioritizing their family responsibilities?

12

You Give Them Something to Eat

Jesus replied, "They do not need to go away.
You give them something to eat."
MATTHEW 14:16, NIV

LIKE ANY INSTITUTION OR ORGANISM, local churches have a life cycle. They are born, grow, and at some later date most will die. It may take a few years or stretch out to a few hundred, but eventually even the best organizations come to an end. Sadly, some local churches die before their time. They prematurely abort their mission and cut short the life spans they could have enjoyed. There are several reasons for this, but a consistent reason for a church's demise almost always lies at the feet of the church's leadership—or, rather, lack of leadership.

While we can critique the response of the disciples and their unwillingness to meet the needs of the hungry congregation, we must applaud their organizational skills to get the job done. Can you imagine the herculean task it must have been to coordinate and execute the mammoth responsibility to feed five thousand men plus their families? Most of us could handle feeding a few dozen people, or we could manage to accommodate upwards of maybe two hundred people. But to satisfy the appetites of fifteen thousand people is by itself a miracle.

I believe the disciples' efficiency in carrying out this impromptu banquet is a consequence of Jesus' leadership in their lives. Jesus would not have asked them to perform this feat unless he knew they possessed the leadership and organizational capability to succeed.

Somehow the disciples were already endowed with gifts of administration, or they observed Jesus' leadership and picked up the skills to lead. Either way, Christ knew they were equipped to do an outstanding job. He gave them a task they could handle.

In our churches, we need to not only identify the needs within our community, but we must also assess the leadership capacity of our congregation to execute and produce results. Ongoing training and development for church leaders is essential for effective ministry. Proper training produces a feeling of empowerment and a willingness to take on more responsibility. If the disciples were not capable of carrying out Christ's request, they would have caused a difficult situation to become even worse. A disorganized process of feeding the thousands would have left the disciples frustrated and the people unfed and unsatisfied. Christ's ministry would have received a poor score on the satisfaction survey by everyone in the crowd.

However, the event was carried out with excellence and proficiency, and everyone received high marks for a job well done. This is not the case in many of our churches. Too often, despite our benevolent desire to serve our community, the recipients of care are left with a bad impression when we muddle through an outreach endeavor with confusing and cumbersome processes that do not serve the people well.

When assisting others, we often do need them to fill out important and pertinent information so that we can document the service and follow up afterward. But the forms do not need to be five to seven pages to get food from our pantries. Nor should the public have to go through three or four different people to get help to buy medicine or to get a gas card to go to work. While we are serving our community, we must keep in mind the emotional and sometimes physical difficulties people may be experiencing when they are asking for help. Therefore, to serve well, we must have simple and straightforward administrative processes.

I recall the first forms we produced years ago when our community reached out to us for assistance. I am ashamed to report that we had a three-page application that required them to provide their Social Security number, two main references, photo ID, and a few other items, just to get bread and a few cans of vegetables. We were being overly cautious because we were aware of persons who prey on churches and charitable organizations to abuse the system.

It didn't take us long to abandon our CIA-level applications and adopt a simpler form that was less burdensome for the clients. We learned to spend more time in conversation with the people than they spent filling out paperwork. The relational connection was the most important aspect of the interaction because we could ascertain the people's real needs. Our goal was to have an opportunity to share Christ with them and not to interrogate them like a governmental agency.

We also had to ensure that our volunteers were properly prepared to serve in this ministry. Those who desired to serve needed more than just a willing heart. They also had to possess a cheerful smile and a positive attitude. Serving people well takes a hefty dose of patience and genuine care for those they serve. People in need often come from a place of brokenness and pain. Some feel ashamed that they need to seek help. Therefore, we must ensure that those who greet them and provide assistance are sensitive to and mindful of their vulnerabilities and challenges.

Those who minister to others must keep in mind that we are servants to the community and that the church's reputation won't be established by how the church responds to the notable and influential people. It will be evaluated by how it handles those Jesus described as "the least of these" in Matthew 25:37-40 (NIV).

> Then the righteous will answer him, "Lord, when did we see you hungry and feed you, or thirsty and give you something to drink? When did we see you a stranger and invite you in, or needing clothes and clothe you? When did we see you sick or in prison and go to visit you?" The King will reply, "Truly I tell you, whatever you did for one of the least of these brothers and sisters of mine, you did for me."

When Jesus characterizes "the least of these," he is speaking of people who are vulnerable in society—the economically disadvantaged, the socially and psychologically challenged, the physically disabled and spiritually defeated. Every church and every staff member and volunteer must believe and embrace the reality that all humans are made in the image of God (Genesis 1:26-27) and therefore have the same intrinsic worth as creatures of value in the sight of God. Congregations must agree to a corporate value system that honors and extends dignity to all.

When this core attitude is rooted in the makeup and personality of the church, it will spread throughout the community, and soon the church will be viewed as a safe place that seeks to serve and where transformation can truly happen. Without it, the surrounding community will choose to avoid the church. It may take years to undo a reputation of being unfriendly, indifferent, and distant.

When people are mishandled, the church would do well to own the mistake quickly. Take full responsibility and do all you can to make it right. Provide ongoing training for church leaders and volunteers in best practices of hospitality and customer service. If it becomes clear that a person—whether paid or unpaid—isn't well suited for a particular role, quickly move him or her to a more appropriate role. This is especially true if the person is required to interact with the public. An inhospitable staff person or volunteer will cost the church exponentially in a very short time.

Senior staff should participate in the church's outreach initiatives from time to time. This will give them an understanding and appreciation for what goes on in the ministry, how efficiently it operates, and what type of relational environment exists among the personnel and toward the people being served. Business schools teach "management by walking around." Jesus did this well as he constantly evaluated the effectiveness of his disciples' work and paid attention to how well they related to each other and to the community.

Most churches are filled with some of the most loving and selfless people on the planet. I know that is true in our church and in most churches I have visited. In every community across our nation, the church should be known as the one place anyone can go to get their needs met.

One of my wife's favorite shows growing up was *Little House on the Prairie*. In recent years, as I watched reruns with her, I noticed one compelling thing about most episodes. The church, centered in the middle of the community, was the place that everyone ran to for almost any issue. That little church and its members provided

Bible-based solutions to many of the issues affecting families and businesses. Today, no one church has all the answers or expertise for every problem that plagues society. But we do have access to greater resources to help us guide people to the right path, and we have access, through prayer, to the God who can do all things. With God's help, we *can* feed them.

> *How effective is the hospitality at your church? Are your documents too complicated when people come for assistance? What can you do to make the experience better for the recipients? How are you having conversations so that you can share Christ with them?*

13

Don't Send People Away

Jesus replied, "They do not need to go away.
You give them something to eat."

MATTHEW 14:16, NIV

THE DISCIPLES WERE IN FAVOR of sending the crowd home. Their feet were tired, their stomachs were empty, and they were worn out from a full day of ministry. They were finished . . . but Jesus was not. He knew there were still those in the assembly who needed something deeper, and he was committed to ensuring that everyone left fulfilled in body, soul, and spirit. So he proclaimed in what I imagine was a chastising tone: "They do not need to go away!"

I wonder who it was in the masses of people who tugged on Jesus' heart. Who at this gathering touched him like the woman with the issue of blood did in Mark 5:31, compelling Jesus to stop and ask, "Who touched me?"

Perhaps it was a family on the brink of destruction and Jesus' words had the power to give them hope. Maybe it was a man contemplating suicide who needed to hear one more sermon from

Christ to find the strength to go on. Possibly Jesus knew the little boy who would give his lunch needed to participate in a miracle that would change his life forever. It is feasible that he extended the event so he could teach an object lesson to his dim-witted disciples. We will never know for whom Jesus extended the time, but we know why he did it. Because every soul matters.

Does every soul matter to you? It matters to Jesus. And it should matter to us. It mattered to four men in Mark 2:1-5:

> When Jesus returned to Capernaum several days later,
> the news spread quickly that he was back home. Soon the
> house where he was staying was so packed with visitors
> that there was no more room, even outside the door.
> While he was preaching God's word to them, four men
> arrived carrying a paralyzed man on a mat. They couldn't
> bring him to Jesus because of the crowd, so they dug a
> hole through the roof above his head. Then they lowered
> the man on his mat, right down in front of Jesus. Seeing
> their faith, Jesus said to the paralyzed man, "My child,
> your sins are forgiven."

We are not told if these four men were the family of the paralyzed man. The Bible does not specify the link of their relationship—it only demonstrates to us the depth of their love and concern for him. We do not know how far they had to travel to carry the man to the packed home. There is no clarity on the relationship they had with each other. They are only connected to the need of this paralyzed man and his hopeless condition without Christ.

They would not allow a closed door or an overflowing crowd to stop them from their mission. Even the cost of repairing the torn roof would not dissuade them. They risked the man's safety by lowering him from the ceiling, and public ridicule from the crowd for acting recklessly. But it was worth it, because every soul matters!

After each sermon I preach (except when my favorite football team, Atlanta, is playing New Orleans at 1:00 p.m.), I come down on the floor to greet, pray for, and minister to whoever needs my time. I get chastised by some who say, "You need to go back to your office, you've done enough after preaching." But no matter how tired I am or covered with sweat after delivering the Word, this is my favorite time. I know I have one more mini-sermon to impart to someone who needs just a little more. I have to close my eyes and pray once more for a family who needs me to stand with them before God's throne. I always hold back a little extra spiritual nugget from my sermon for these special times. I can't send them away. Because every soul counts.

Over fifteen years ago, our church rented out a lake one Sunday to have a church picnic. We had bouncy houses for the kids, games for the adults, and an abundance of down-home southern barbecue. The highlight of the event was the public baptism of about twenty people in the lake. We had two baptism lines to speed the process because the cooks were calling us all to the table. The whole congregation joined around the area, we sang, and I shared about the meaning of baptism and the new life we receive when we give ourselves to Christ.

Among the twenty candidates were two young sisters. Once they were baptized, their older brother, who had come to witness the event, yelled out, "How do I do that?" I passionately explained how to give your life to Christ, and to everyone's delight he accepted Christ standing on the shoreline. He immediately asked to be baptized. And with all his street clothes on, he jumped in to be immersed in the water and rose with a huge smile that sent the crowd into a frenzy.

I am so glad we didn't tell him to wait till we got back to church and do it the following week. I'm so thankful we didn't send him away because he was not properly dressed in our white baptism robes and had no change of clothes for the day. We didn't send him away. Because every soul matters.

I relay this story because of what transpired next. Late the next evening, I got a call from the young man's mother. She was frantic and sobbing. She said her son hadn't come home the previous night, and she was not able to reach him all day. The following day she filed a missing person report, and over the next few days everyone searched for him until we received the disturbing news that he had been murdered.

The police had video footage of him walking toward a warehouse near one of Atlanta's subway train stations with two other men. But moments later, only the other two returned. Police canvassed the area and discovered that he had been shot in the warehouse. When the police arrested the assailants, they gave an astonishing reason for his murder.

When he had returned home from our church's picnic and baptism at the lake, he was excited about his new relationship with Christ and vowed to radically change his life as a new Christian. He belonged to a local street gang and shared his decision with the principal leaders of the gang. They reported that he refused to renounce his association with Christ. The more they insisted that he disown the Lord, the more he held on to his faith and would not surrender his conviction.

The gang members were afraid he would give up their secrets and betray them if he continued following Jesus, so they forced him to make a choice. With only one day as a Christian, he stood up to the pressure. And like a seasoned first-century disciple, he allowed them to kill his body because Christ possessed his soul. He was a martyr for the faith without ever attending Sunday school, joining a church, or memorizing Scripture.

Days later we held his funeral. Hundreds of teenagers from his school attended and heard the story of his conversion. Several gave their lives to Christ, and some are still in our church and serve Christ faithfully. His mother and family became charter members in one of the churches we planted. And in my office, I have a framed picture of his baptism. It depicts him coming out of the water flanked by two of our ministers.

I keep that picture on my wall to remind me that every soul matters. Each Sunday before I leave my office to go to the pulpit, I glance at that picture. It reminds me not to be consumed with time, obstacles, or any distractions that may emerge. I secretly whisper a prayer and trust that God has brought to our church that day someone who needs to discern the movement of God's Spirit. I commit to walk slowly through the crowd and, like Jesus, make certain that to the best of my ability, no one is sent away without their needs met.

Remembering that every soul matters is what drives our staff and volunteers. It is the secret sauce that makes our church special.

My prayer for you and your ministry is that you will experience similar expressions of God's grace.

Take time now to pray for someone God places on your heart. Ask God for an opportunity to share your salvation story with them. Put an item or a picture of a person you are praying for on your desk at work, in your car, or on your refrigerator to remind you that every soul matters.

Dave Travis Interview

Dave has a wealth of experience from both pastoral ministry and the business world. He has worked as a pastor and has consulted with many churches in different contexts, including recovery ministry. Through Leadership Network he has learned from many esteemed mentors. His involvement in this network has given him opportunities to work with ministries all over the country.

Tyrone Barnette

Tell me about your career in Christian leadership. You have been used greatly to assist thousands of churches over the years.

Dave Travis

Well, you and I first met when I was the associational missionary at Stone Mountain Baptist Association. I then joined an organization called Leadership Network and worked with large churches in the United States, Canada, and Europe for about twenty-four years. I retired in 2018. Now I serve an organization called Generis, where I primarily work with senior pastors in strategic planning for their churches and for their succession plans and with their boards. So that's kind of what I do.

Tyrone Barnette

Excellent. Well, you do a great job, and I can appreciate your friendship. You've been in my life almost my entire spiritual life. What trends do you see related to outreach and evangelism, and given the pandemic, are there any things we need to do differently now?

Dave Travis

What I see is not a great emphasis on evangelism, which I think is a huge mistake. Each church will have its own unique ministry, depending on its community, its constituency, and who the people and their pastor are best equipped to reach.

During the pandemic, many of the digital outreach strategies really worked and should continue to work. As you probably know, it used to be that nobody in the recovery movement thought that online would work. And now, to everyone's surprise, it works. I'm not saying that should be our sole focus in recovery ministry. But reaching people online has worked for meetings and accountability. I believe there will be a greater need for recovery and mental health ministries in the future, and online ministry will be the catalyst for growth.

Your book references the feeding of the five thousand, and it demonstrates that it doesn't take a lot of resources to reach the community. It takes committed people willing to invest in the lives of others and to risk it getting messy. Churches will discover new ways to do more with less and how to leverage resources beyond tithes and offerings.

The other thing concerning the feeding of the five thousand is that it wasn't just Jesus who produced the miracle. He told the twelve disciples to sit the people down in groups to distribute the food, and it wasn't until the end when they realized the miracle had occurred. We need to help pastors and leaders know that they may not see the results of their labor until the work is done. Just be consistent and committed.

At the same time, the pandemic and related effects have caused a lot of people to reevaluate their lives. What am I doing with my life? What am I doing with my career? What am I doing with my family? We need to just be bold and encourage people to take big leaps and make big commitments. We need to call people to make commitments to Christ because people won't take a step unless you ask them. We have to give them clear direction. Then show what the next step in commitment is for them. Churches need to design ministries with that in mind.

I think this will lead the church to raise up spiritual mentors who will walk alongside someone they are assigned to. When someone joins the church, the next step is to connect them with one of our spiritual mentors, not in a class or program. They're going to be in touch almost like with a sponsor in AA or for a recovery ministry. They are going to talk several times a week. They will be just a friend walking together with them, helping them to grow in their faith. This can happen either in person or virtually. I had a couple of churches during the pandemic that grew this way. Younger generations in particular crave mentorship or spiritual fathering, or spiritual mothering. This will be a greater trend in the future.

Tyrone Barnette

How receptive do you think the unchurched are to the gospel today? Do you think there's a resistance, and if so, why?

Dave Travis

The culture is not bending our way. And we shouldn't expect it to. Even when the culture did kind of bend our way, it was often lip service. We say that people are resistant to the gospel, but they may only be resistant to how we're presenting it. Most people believe there is at least some kind of higher power or spiritual force in the world. They just don't know how to access God, and it's our job to show them.

Tyrone Barnette

You work with hundreds of churches and pastors in all types of denominations. What should pastors be focused on now?

Dave Travis

Well, the way I say it is: What is the story of hope, and how do we present the gospel in a way that's relevant to the communities in which we're serving? That looks different for every community.

Two churches will have the same story of the gospel, but the way they communicate it may look different.

Tyrone Barnette

What would you say that church planters should do differently than a pastor with a five-hundred-member congregation?

Dave Travis

Church planters must work personally and individually with lots of people, especially in the early days of the new venture. Church planters should be going into apartment complexes and housing units, grocery stores, and other places to build personal relationships with the people in the community. They should want to hear people's stories. They should be saying, "We want to be your friends here, and we'll help connect you to our best friend, Jesus. We want to know where you're coming from spiritually." I think those other things are what we should have been saying all along, instead of just saying, "Well, let me tell you about Jesus." We often have the gift of listening in evangelism and can begin by saying, "Tell me your story," because that reveals to us what their needs are and where we can help.

The church planter does more personal, individual work in the community, whereas the church of five hundred should be working with teams of people to do a variety of outreach and evangelism projects.

14

Here I Am. Send Me.

Jesus said, "You feed them."
MARK 6:37

I HAVE KNOWN PASTORS who have faithfully served their churches for years. They are insightful teachers and powerful preachers of God's Word. Each faithfully spends hours studying the Scriptures to deliver a life-changing message every Sunday. Their personal lives are beyond reproach as they lovingly provide for their families and care for their congregations. By all standards, they are models of excellence.

However, I constantly challenge these pastors on their reluctance to leave the church office and spend time in the community. As a result of this reluctance, their churches have been stalled for some time and have declined significantly since the pandemic. Yet, it is still a struggle to get these pastors to spend more time connecting to their communities. They are of the belief that all they need to do is preach and teach the Word and the people will come. Sadly, the members of their congregations have adopted this relaxed view of evangelism and rarely engage the community. Their attitude is derived from an extreme theological conviction that God has already chosen who should be saved and there is nothing they can do to alter the destinies of those who are not the elect.

So my pastor friends have no problem embracing the view and attitude of the disciples, who say, "Send the people away." In their defense, they certainly feel the pain of the community and are troubled by the sinful and corrupt lifestyles they witness in their respective neighborhoods. But they do not believe that they must go to any extra lengths to offer Christ to people. They simply wait on God to send lost people to the church whenever God determines it is their time to hear. As a result of this belief system, these pastors see little value in evangelism.

I absolutely believe in the sovereignty of God. The Bible proclaims the sovereignty of God over all creation. Nebuchadnezzar declares in Daniel 4:34-35:

> I, Nebuchadnezzar, looked up to heaven. My sanity
> returned, and I praised and worshiped the Most High and
> honored the one who lives forever. His rule is everlasting,
> and his kingdom is eternal. All the people of the earth are
> nothing compared to him. He does as he pleases among
> the angels of heaven and among the people of the earth.
> No one can stop him or say to him, "What do you mean
> by doing these things?"

But Scripture also places the responsibility on every Christian to do whatever we can to proclaim the gospel and lead people into a relationship with Jesus. Paul shares his passion in 1 Corinthians 9:16:

> Yet preaching the Good News is not something I can
> boast about. I am compelled by God to do it. How
> terrible for me if I didn't preach the Good News!

Paul says he is compelled by God to share the gospel. He goes even further in Romans 1:14-15 when he says he is *obligated* to share his faith in Christ:

> For I have a great sense of obligation to people in both
> the civilized world and the rest of the world, to the
> educated and uneducated alike. So I am eager to come to
> you in Rome, too, to preach the Good News.

I believe that individuals and churches are expected to do more than preach the gospel from pulpits or simply bring up Christ in casual conversations with neighbors and friends. We must develop and launch programs and produce strategies to intentionally extend the gospel to as many people as possible. We must use creative and engaging approaches to earn us the right for people to open their minds and hearts to our message.

God has called and appointed every believer to the work of evangelism. The Great Commission of Matthew 28:19-20 wasn't just a directive for clergy but for each of us. Our diligence in carrying out Christ's command has eternal consequences for each person we meet. The fact that our lack of obedience could adversely affect someone's eternal destiny should burden our hearts and motivate us not to waste one day or minimize any encounter. We must "make the most of every opportunity in these evil days" (Ephesians 5:16).

Each of us can confidently fulfill this assignment because God has equipped us with all we need to complete the task. "God is able to make all grace abound to you, so that having all suffi-ciency in all things at all times, you may abound in every good work" (2 Corinthians 9:8, ESV). Furthermore, in 2 Corinthians 12:9 (NIV), he reassures us, "My grace is sufficient for you, for my power is made perfect in weakness." So take pleasure in knowing that God not only calls us to share the gospel but gives us the tools, skills, opportunities, and power to achieve his divine pur-pose when we are willing to offer ourselves to him.

My most memorable encounters with God's Spirit have been when I'm in a conversation with someone who doesn't know Christ. You can sense God's Spirit creating windows and doors of opportu-nity as he builds bridges from their pain to his hope. It is remarkable how uncomplicated witnessing can be when there is a dependence on the Lord. Every believer has been equipped to witness to the world, despite the walls that separate people by age, gender, or culture.

In Acts 2, the Lord gave those gathered in the upper room the power to present the gospel so that everyone present from around the world could understand it in their own language. No mat-ter what linguistic, cultural, or ethnic differences existed, miracu-lously each person heard the message, understood it, and in many cases, responded to it. The Bible records that three thousand souls surrendered to Christ on that day.

I firmly believe God still gives us his Spirit to translate the gospel in a way that others can embrace its truth and experience its power. No, I am not advocating for a debate on glossolalia or whether this is a gift that is still active today. But what I am advo-cating for is that we learn to yield to God's Spirit. When we do, he can give us the ability to minister to someone with whom we have little to no identification.

God can give a fifty-five-year-old white male from the suburbs the ability to speak in the language of a twenty-two-year-old drug addict and win him to Christ. He can empower a Hispanic woman raised in San Antonio, Texas, to speak in the language of a Black teen girl raised on the streets of Harlem, New York. The Christian businessman can relate and communicate with the homeless man outside his office, and the southern farmer can make a spiritual connection with the gothic punk rocker reared on the streets of Venice Beach, California. When we are endowed with God's Spirit and his power, we can cross cultural boundary lines and relate to persons who are vastly different from us, not unlike the disciples on the Day of Pentecost.

It is God's will that his children share and explain his love to a world that is lost and dying. The world needs us, and God will use you if you make yourself available.

Saying we are called to reach the world sounds overwhelming and out of reach. But when we reach the world through the life of the one person God is sending us to, we are fulfilling the Great Commission.

I've taught my church to expect God to put someone on their heart to pray for; and when the opportunity arises to share Christ with that person, to trust that they will also be given what they need to say or do. And the Holy Spirit will make their message clear to the person they speak with. This is how we partner with the Holy Spirit. It is not a sales pitch, negotiation, debate, or the peddling of a heavenly life insurance plan. Evangelism has more to do with building relationships than trying to build a convincing case for Christianity.

Don't send the people away as the disciples attempted to do. Consider that God has provided you an open door of opportunity to make connections. Don't just sit in your office or stay huddled in the church building ministering to one another. Believe that God has equipped you with all you need and that when you are open and available, God will use you in ways beyond your imagination. Claim the promise God gave Jeremiah: "Then the LORD put forth His hand and touched my mouth, and the LORD said to me: 'Behold, I have put My words in your mouth'" (Jeremiah 1:9, NKJV).

Don't send the people away. Instead, adopt the attitude of Isaiah and say to the Lord, "Here I am. Send me" (Isaiah 6:8).

Pray that the Lord will send you to someone with whom you have no natural affinity. Ask God's Spirit to give you the ability to relate to them as you share your faith and tell them your salvation story.

Lee May Interview

In 2006, Lee entered the world of politics by running for the DeKalb County Commission in Georgia. In 2013, he was appointed chief executive officer for DeKalb County. In both positions, Lee was and remains the youngest person in either role in the county's history.

In 2017, Pastor Lee answered the call of God to plant a church. With his wife, Robin, and a small yet powerful team, he planted Transforming Faith Church in Stonecrest, Georgia.

Tyrone Barnette

You planted your church a few years ago, just before the pandemic. How do you see your approach to evangelism and outreach differently than a pastor in an established church that's been in the community a long time? Are there things you must do differently?

Lee May

I think the biggest difference is, as a church planter, we are mandated and have no choice but to live out Matthew 28:19 [ASV], "Go ye therefore, and make disciples." Because as a church planter, no one knows us. We have to go tell people prayerfully about our Christ but also introduce ourselves and then try to figure out how to make some connection in order to do life with them. That is a little different from an established church that has been in the community for a long time and already has roots in the community.

Tyrone Barnette

I tell pastors who are trying to reengage with the community following this pandemic that they need to think like a church planter. What advice can you give them?

Lee May

Well, the pandemic made us all rethink what church looks like. Two years into our church starting, the world shut down. We were just figuring out what it means to be a church. And then we had to automatically shift and adjust how we did things. I think being a church planter makes it easier, because we didn't even have a staff. We were worshiping in a school, and we didn't have some of the fixed costs and fixed expenses that established churches have. Nor did we have a lot of the expectations that people have about what a church should be doing. We already knew we had to be creative. I think what established churches need to do is become more creative and learn to pivot like a church planter when things change suddenly and unexpectedly.

One of the good things about being a church planter is that typically your membership is younger in age. So we had a younger congregation, who were also accustomed to technology, streaming online, giving online. The transition, I think, was really good. I would encourage an established church to embrace the younger generation and technology to advance their church in this new paradigm.

I would say the other difference between us and established churches is that we couldn't rely on our history. We couldn't rely on our programs. Our focus was to get into the lives of people and figure out how we could be a blessing to them. I think established churches can learn from us church planters how to recast their visions to do outreach.

For us, outreach has always been big from day one. How can we find a tangible need? How do we enter into people's lives to make a difference? How do we not only say we love God, but that we genuinely love God's people and demonstrate it in tangible ways?

Tyrone Barnette

Some of the greatest and most effective evangelistic successes are being accomplished by new churches. Most of the older established churches get stuck in programs and traditions, whereas church plants seek out innovation and take risks that result in a higher baptism rate than established congregations. I planted our church thirty years ago, and I still have a romantic crush on my early days of church planting.

Lee May

I've learned to say, if you just stay faithful and be consistent where God has you, you will eventually get to where you believe God wants you to go. And we just have to stay loyal to that, even if it's not in our own timing.

Tyrone Barnette

What are some of the innovative things you've done as a church planter to reach your community?

Lee May

In our school district, there were kids who had negative lunch balances at school. The school would still allow the children to eat even if they didn't have money. For a while, they'd allow the balances to rack up, and the student could eat what everyone else ate at lunch. But at some point, the balance would get too high. The school would still feed them but shift to a lesser meal, like a peanut butter and jelly sandwich. It would be embarrassing because it was clear to everyone what was going on.

So we decided to step forward and see what we could do to wipe out the negative lunch balances for elementary school kids and their parents. We called it our generosity campaign, and we were able to raise money and wipe away negative school lunch balances of twenty-four elementary schools in the district.

The families were grateful, and we gained some visibility in the community.

When you give the school district anything above $5,000, the school board has to vote to receive it, per their policy. So I had to attend their board meeting. They were so grateful, and they began to talk about our church as if it were a megachurch. I had to stop them and say, "Look, I want you to know that what we are giving today has come from a church with a membership of sixty-eight people," which is what we were at the time.

We're a small church, but we have big, very generous hearts. Generosity is one of our core values. We say at our church, "Pound for pound, we will be the most generous church around."

Now remember, we start off with asking, What is the real need in our community? And how can we make a difference? So we've just kind of shifted and started looking for other areas in need. There are extended-stay hotels and motels around our county that are homes where people live year-round. And school buses drive to these hotels when school starts and pick up kids in these situations. So we've decided to target our back-to-school giveaways to some of those local hotels in South DeKalb County. We're collecting tennis shoes for kids and some other things, toiletries and items that they need. Any size church can make a big difference if they just look around and see what hurting people need.

Tyrone Barnette

This book is based on the feeding of the five thousand. Jesus took sardines and crackers and was able to feed approximately fifteen thousand people. He just used what he had. We can do the same.

You stepped away from politics after serving as the CEO of DeKalb County, with a population of 750,000 residents, to plant the church that you're serving now. Was it easier serving as the

CEO of the county or as a church planter? Are there differences and similarities?

Lee May

It's different. Being in politics as a commissioner and a CEO, I felt like this was my ministry. I felt like this was God's call on my life. I felt like the county was my congregation. I used to tell my dad, who always was eager for me to pastor, "I've got the biggest church in America. I've got 750,000 loyal tithers because they pay taxes. As a matter of fact, we get it first."

The ministry and the marketplace are just different. For the county, I oversaw a billion-dollar budget, and more than one thousand employees. Today, as a church planter, I have fewer resources, fewer people, a smaller staff. But I realize I can make a difference one person at a time, in small pockets of communities at a time. The church and I can make a difference there.

Tyrone Barnette

Thank you for sharing that. God is calling men and women out of the marketplace, just as Jesus did with his disciples. I love how you viewed your secular work as a ministry that was just as important as your church assignment. If more people could take that approach and view their jobs as a ministry assignment and calling, we could turn this world upside down by proclaiming Jesus is Lord on Sundays at eleven o'clock and Monday through Friday, nine to five.

15

Better Together: Forming Partnerships

Jesus said, "You feed them."

"With what?" they asked. "We'd have to work for months to earn enough money to buy food for all these people!"

MARK 6:37

IT NEVER OCCURRED TO THE DISCIPLES to invite others to come alongside them and link up with someone else to meet the colossal need of feeding five thousand men plus their families. It's doubtful that there was someone or some organization nearby who could have assisted them. I can't imagine there would have been a first-century Chick-fil-A or Walmart nearby. Yet, the Bible doesn't share with us that they even considered partnering with someone until Jesus mentioned it.

Not wanting to ask for help or seek viable partnerships is a limitation of many church leaders. We somehow equate asking for help as a sign of weakness or a mark of our incompetence. That frontiersman mentality to go it alone is rooted in an independent streak that is a feature of the American church. We have not been taught to partner and cooperate with others, which hinders our ability to achieve greater results.

One reason we do not care to form partnerships is that we cherish the idea that we did something alone and therefore can receive the credit for the accomplishment. Sharing glory is not a characteristic of the modern church. We allow our competitive nature to make us apprehensive of others who could add considerable value to our efforts if we were willing to bring them aboard.

It amazes me how many churches are within walking distance of each other and rarely, if ever, do ministry together to reach their collective community. Each church has a food pantry, clothing closet, similar support groups, and other basic programs to minister to the community. What would happen if they combined their energies and merged some of their offerings to make a much greater impact?

If there is any organization on earth that should be able to work together and cooperate, it should be the church. In fact, Christ calls and expects us to work together. In Mark 6:7, Jesus sends his disciples out two by two as partners. He doesn't want us to do ministry alone.

When we combine our faith and works, there is nothing we can't do. And think of the incredible witness it is to the neighborhood or city when churches unite to undertake some community-transforming venture. The message it sends places a spotlight on Jesus and is a stark contrast to what is seen in our world, where we compete with one another rather than complete each other. Our unity communicates Christ's love, humility, and power to bring about change. It can become a graphic illustration for the unchurched to open their minds and hearts and believe Jesus can bring wholeness to their lives.

To set up partnerships, one church needs to take the initiative and make the first move. You may be surprised how eager some other church may be about the idea of partnership. When you plan your outreach events and community programs, consider asking another local church to participate with you. Do website searches to find out what other ministries are doing and check to see if they are open to collaborate. If they are, then set up a meeting and imagine what you can do together to engage the community.

When our church has done this, we have experienced tremendous success. Once we partnered to put on a Fourth of July event with other churches. Food, fireworks, and fellowship were multiplied when we combined our efforts. Best of all, we saw thousands of people attend and dozens yield their lives to Christ as a result. The new converts had several churches to choose from as they started their new Christian journey. More than a few times, attendees remarked on the cooperative spirit that existed between the churches of different races, denominations, and sizes.

Working with other congregations generates more volunteers, more financial resources, and greater creativity. It also allows the church to have effective ministry offerings throughout the year. For instance, one church may host the Fall Festival or food pantry at their site, and another may provide the space for a clothing closet or Easter Extravaganza on their property. This allows both churches to multiply the number of ministry projects they provide for a given year without investing double the resources of people and funds because of the collaboration. And as an added benefit, both churches can offer ministry to the community throughout the year instead of just in one season.

Partnering with other churches, especially if they are in close proximity to each other, is risky and takes a God-sized degree of humility and servanthood. But the benefits outweigh the challenges. One church may take the lead for one project, while the other church takes the lead for the next one. The budget, space, volunteers, and follow-up planning should be handled in advance, with a small group of representatives from both congregations, to anticipate obstacles and manage expectations.

Churches can also partner with various faith-based and secular organizations to advance their missions. However, churches should never form partnerships that compromise their core belief in Christ or severely vacate the church's values and integrity. In later chapters, we will examine how to form and administer partnerships with secular and governmental groups. For now, we will look at partnering with faith-based groups that align with the church's beliefs and values.

In my experience, partnering with like-minded, faith-based parachurch organizations has been a remarkable benefit to our ministry over the years. From my earliest days as a church planter, forming partnerships was essential to our survival. We shared buildings with churches that generously allowed us to have space at a low cost in their facilities. We joined with larger churches to start food pantries, recovery ministries, and youth programs. With each new partner we learned how to do ministry, and to this day the principles we learned from those congregations and parachurch organizations drive much of what we do.

Even though we were smaller in those early days, we exerted a lot of influence on the partner church or organization that was larger and more skilled than we were. As small as we were, we brought to the table resources, experiences, connections to the community, and insight the partner did not possess. A true partnership should be mutually beneficial to both groups. The larger and more resourceful party must be aware of the tendency to become paternalistic and controlling. Likewise, the less resourced partner must not develop an unhealthy dependency that can handicap them in the future.

If the partner is a faith-based organization and not a church, I suggest that the primary driver of the relationship be the local church. While there are some amazing and essential nonprofits that work in the Kingdom of God, God has called the church to carry out his mandate to reach the world. Faith-based organizations should work through the church to assist the church in fulfilling its mission. That is not to say that a church has all the answers or calls all the shots, but the partnership with the agency should have a default thinking that is always focused on how to keep the church's work central in the community and throughout the world. The church is the conduit of ongoing evangelism, discipleship, and fellowship. The church is the spiritual covering for the community and any organization it works with.

What partnerships do you have that are mutually beneficial? What partnerships do you need to form to reach your community? Are there other churches in your community that you could partner with on some project? Are there some partnerships you need to discontinue?

16

Serving with Limited Resources

"We have here only five loaves of bread and two fish," they answered.
MATTHEW 14:17, NIV

THE DISCIPLES FELT DEFEATED. They had solicited an offering from the five thousand and only received five loaves of bread and two fish. This result would have been a letdown for any church after such a powerful day of teaching and fellowship. The needs of the crowd eclipsed this small contribution, and there seemed no reasonable way these puny resources could meet the demand. It seemed sensible to limit any further expansion of ministry and to halt any new programming. Expansion was just not in the budget, someone could argue.

Every church ministry, no matter how large or small, must contend with the challenge of limited resources. The lack of funds has killed many visions and stalled countless initiatives that would have made a significant difference in the lives of others. Very few leaders are eager to bankrupt the church's treasury to chase an idea that may result in them receiving a pink slip and a U-Haul truck.

So, for most, the budget rules the day and tells the church how much of the community it can reach and what innovative activities it can deploy to change the world.

But money shouldn't dictate what the church can and cannot do. It is a tool that, if leveraged correctly, can assist the church in reaching its full potential. The church should be steered by God, a compelling vision, and the Good Book, not its financial ledger. Too many pastors believe their problems could be solved if they could just have a bigger budget. They do not realize that money is seldom the problem for a church when the focus remains on evangelism and discipleship.

Proper stewardship begins with an understanding that everything we possess belongs to God. If the vision for the church and its community has been bathed in prayer and carried out as a directive from God, then trust that what God initiates, he sustains. I tell my church, "Where God guides, God will provide." We have witnessed this throughout the thirty years of my ministry at Peace Baptist. Time and time again, God has made resources available to carry out his vision for our church in phenomenal ways. The question is not, Is it in the budget? The question should always be, Is this the will of God?

I'm not trying to be super spiritual, or foolhardy, suggesting that we shouldn't plan or make sure there are adequate resources to complete a task once it is launched (Luke 14:28). But I earnestly want to call God's people back to trusting him with what we have. Too often in the contemporary church, we have exchanged our faith in God for business practices that box God out of solutions. I want to challenge the church to believe that God can and will provide.

He is still feeding the five thousand with crackers and sardines. He gives creativity and vision to leaders who seek his divine guidance. I could not write this book and not encourage you to trust God for provision for your church.

This is not to say that you do not need to be pragmatic, full of integrity, and wise in how you handle money. It is not proper to mismanage funds and blame your failures and shortsightedness on following God by faith. He expects us to render to Caesar what is Caesar's (Mark 12:17) and to be diligent in all our financial stewardship. A church's financial standing is not an indicator of a church's success, but mishandling resources is a direct indicator of a church's failure.

There is possibly no church in the world that has not had to wrestle with the reality that faced the disciples on that fateful day. They faced enormous need and were willing to meet the need, but they lacked the proper resources to complete the job. With only two fish and five loaves of bread, it was reasonable to conclude that there was not enough.

Those of us who sit in boardrooms to strategize on various ministry projects have had to confront the sobering fact that there is never enough money to do what we are being called to do. There is much more faith than finance. More willingness than wealth. More motivation than the means to succeed. This awareness of limited resources stifles innovation and ingenuity. It causes us to keep our Spirit-birthed dreams God shares with us safely tucked in our hearts. We dare not speak them out loud because the bottom line of the budget puts a muzzle on us. Many God-inspired projects and plans never see the light of day because we allow money, or the lack of it, to dictate what we can do for God and our community.

I must applaud the disciples for having the courage to bring the five loaves and two fish to Jesus. They presented the lunch of the little boy and dared to believe that somehow Jesus could do something with it. Perhaps Jesus' followers thought they could at least demonstrate to the crowd that they tried to provide a meal with little results. Their actions inspire me and motivate me to do the same. Our choice is to either come to Christ with the best we have or stand before him empty-handed.

Unfortunately, in my younger days of pastoring, I often acted as if my hands were empty. When I conducted board meetings and church business meetings with the congregation, I was afraid to share a substantial vision that would take a considerable amount of money to achieve. Instead, I would dwarf the vision so that it could fit securely in the church's budget. I allowed the lack of funds to silence my faith and subvert my leadership and the advancement of the church.

Over time, I have been less reluctant to keep ideas and dreams to myself. I've learned two things over the years about sharing vision. I've learned to trust the leaders around me and believe they can hear God's voice too. And secondly, I've learned that money should rarely be an obstacle to advancing God's mission. Whether it is in the budget or not, it costs nothing to share the dream with other visionary leaders and explore the possibility of it being realized.

Some of our best projects and plans came to life when we sat in boardrooms or around the living-room table asking each other, *What if?* We have developed the same faith of the disciples and are not afraid to bring to Jesus our five loaves and two fish. We are comfortable having our ideas shot down or even challenged. Now, at our leadership meetings, no brainstorming notion or inspiration is off-limits, except arguing at the start that there isn't enough money.

When you begin to have discussions to explore ministry initiatives and projects, do not allow the resources in the church's treasury to frame the discussion. It will curtail a robust dialogue and minimize the possibilities of what can be done. The lack of resources has the ability to stifle creative thinking and suppress outside-of-the-box solutions.

A few years ago, our church had a dream of radically serving the public schools in our area. We dreamed of difference-making after-school and summer enrichment programs. Many of the schools in our area were on the State of Georgia's list for improvement and possible takeover. The students were not doing well on tests from elementary to high school. We knew that the parents with kids in the greatest need could not afford the cost of the high-quality program we wanted to offer. We desired a curriculum that would do more than tutor, supplementing their education and exposing them to other activities and experiences outside our urban community. We wanted to take them on trips and teach robotics and computer studies, along with extracurricular activities that would stimulate their minds.

Our team started with this vision and designed the whole program without a consideration of cost. And we wanted the program to be free to the parents who were already dealing with financial challenges. We planned to give the students the level of support some of the for-profit programs provided. Once the entire project was designed, we discovered it would cost more than $300,000 a year to operate for 150 students daily after school and for ten hours a day over the summer. There was no program that served elementary to high school at no cost to parents. We were determined that it was possible, however, and we shared our dream and plans with others.

It wasn't long before we formed a partnership with Sylvan Learning Center to offer our daily, cost-free program to 120 students. God sent us gifted leaders like Gwen Sims and Debbie Miller. They trained our staff and helped us secure funding for our program. Today, we still operate the program year-round and have received well over a million dollars in funding. Best of all, the schools we partner with have been taken off the improvement list and are performing at a higher level than ever before. This never would have happened if we had allowed the lack of funds to cause us to limit our program to a once-a-week tutoring program.

Churches want to see their communities changed and transformed, but it will take funding to make that happen. Churches must make a higher priority of underwriting in the budget the outreach ministry of the church. Sadly, church budgets rarely show a commitment to outreach.

I want to encourage you to make plans and dream about what you believe God wants to do through your church. Write out a job description for a staff position for outreach even if there is no budget for such a role. Once you have the position developed, find a volunteer or two who will operate and take on some of the ministry responsibilities until you are able to hire someone to be on staff.

Develop a missions and outreach mobilization team if your church does not have one. Task them to come up with projects and opportunities that the church can do to reach the community. Let them dream and create plans without allowing financial constraints to hinder them from dreaming. Make sure the senior leader is working with them and that they meet at least monthly for six months. Share their ideas and outcomes with the governing body of the church and create a plan for what projects could be implemented over the following year. All the while the church should be praying for God to clarify his plan and empower the church to reach its community and the world.

Don't let limited resources guide the church or control how much it can do. Certainly, be wise in making plans and be faithful stewards over the finances God has entrusted to your church. But don't be afraid to dream and bring your two fish and five loaves to Christ, and watch the miracle of multiplication transform you, your church, and your community.

Mark DeYmaz Interview

Mark DeYmaz is the founding pastor of the Mosaic Church of Central Arkansas. He is a contributing editor for Outreach *magazine and* Leadership Journal. *He is also a cofounder and executive director of the Mosaix Global Network, an organization dedicated to inspiring unity and diversity in the local church throughout North America and beyond. He authored* Disruption: Repurposing the Church to Redeem the Community; The Coming Revolution in Church Economics; *and* Building a Healthy Multi-Ethnic Church.

Tyrone Barnette

I've enjoyed the books you've written, especially *Disruption*. Can you give me a quick synopsis of what "repurposing the church to redeem the community" entails?

Mark DeYmaz:

People use the word *disruption* in all types of ways. But I'm using it in the business sense, established by Clayton Christensen at the Harvard Business School in 1996. He asked, Why do companies get to the top of their growth curve and then stagnate or decline? There were several hypotheses, such as mismanagement or arrogance, but none of those were the main reasons. The number one reason companies stagnate is that they pay attention to their current customers.

Stated another way, the worst thing a company can do at the top of its growth curve is continue to serve and cater to the customers they already have. If you want to remain credible and relevant, and continue to advance, you must continually reinvent yourself. You have to start a new S curve [a way to measure increasing innovation], a new growth journey. That doesn't mean you have to ditch everything you've done. But you can't just continue to manage your existing business. Because as soon as you do that, you begin to stagnate and decline—and you won't even know it. So you have to start a new S curve and move forward on new product development or open new markets, new doors, new possibilities, etc.

What's true for a company is also true for a church. In *Disruption*, I basically define, address, and apply that thinking to the American church. And man are we in trouble! Most pastors in America, I believe, are doing little more than managing decline right now. More often than not, they're afraid to reinvent themselves, because they're afraid they will lose members or lose money. So they try to protect what they have, and that's the worst thing you can do.

I look at it from a biblical perspective. In John 15, Jesus says every now and then the branch has to be cut back to bear more fruit. I think that's a biblical statement of disruption. Every single church in America was forced to reinvent during the COVID-19 pandemic, and many of them didn't make it. Even now, many people are trying to get back to what they had, but that's the worst thing you could do. You've got to become something new. I don't care if you've been around 150 years or 80 years or 8 years, you have to think with the mindset of a church planter and reinvent. So long story short, that's what the general concept of *Disruption* is about.

One of the best ways to think about our local churches is to become like an American football team. In American football, you have three teams playing simultaneously: offense, defense, and special teams. Those are three separate teams playing three separate games, with three separate metrics, with three separate coaches, but playing synergistically so that the macro team wins.

The way I laid it out shows we need spiritual, social, and financial teams in the American church. I suggest that every church needs to go from a one-dimensional strategy to a three-dimensional strategy. And the spiritual church needs to become more reflective of the Kingdom of God, providing the spiritual offensive strategies of evangelism, discipleship, baptism, etc. That's the spiritual playbook. Then develop a nonprofit or effective outreach program as the social defensive playbook. Finally, special teams become the financial strategy so that the spiritual offense and evangelistic defense have the resources needed to do their work.

Tyrone Barnette

Excellent. How does that look in your church? Are there a couple of examples you can give to help us see how these three teams work together?

Mark DeYmaz

We recently celebrated our twentieth anniversary, and we have a healthy, multiethnic, spiritual church. We do all we can to play our part in the spiritual game with worship, children's ministry, visiting people in the hospital when they're sick, etc. Anything you can think of that a church typically does to meet spiritual needs. We think of those things as like an offensive playbook.

The social playbook is our nonprofit called Vine and Village, where Christ is the vine intersecting the village. Currently, we have nine programs under that umbrella with an executive director and separate board. In our case, we own a total of 100,000 square feet of an old Kmart, and we rent about 45,000 square feet to a major fitness club. Thus, on the church side, we operate out of about 55,000 square feet.

Vine and Village oversees all nine programs. I didn't want to create nine nonprofits, because that would mean nine boards, nine tax returns, nine phone lines, nine copiers, nine websites. So we created an umbrella nonprofit. We can add and subtract programs as needed within that one nonprofit.

For instance, we have the largest food distribution in Little Rock, where 67 percent of our zip code depends on the church for four to five days of meals per month. It's the third largest food network in central Arkansas. With that program we also distribute clothes to hundreds of people every week.

Under the nonprofit, we have an award-winning, internationally known chess program to mentor at-risk kids and teach them critical-thinking skills and reading. They win awards all the time. They pivoted to online during the pandemic, and they crushed it, beating countries from around the world. They're just very good. So that's one program.

We have an immigration law firm and a counseling center. We've operated that for fifteen years and have served more than twelve thousand people. We also rent about 5,000 square feet to Restore Hope Arkansas, a major nonprofit that works with murderers, sex offenders, and others who get out of prison here in Arkansas. It's funded by our governor and the state. They also operate our county's Resource Center out of there too. So we run that in partnership with them.

We also have a trucking school that teaches people how to drive trucks—with all kinds of programs and services for people getting out of prison who need a job they can qualify for. All of this is the social defense playbook.

The third playbook is the financial side. We were attracted to the inner city, where our church is located, so we leveraged space in a well-known fitness center and gave them low rent. Now six thousand people have joined at ten dollars a month. It's a very successful, effective health club that is as good as anything in the suburbs. And I already mentioned the 5,000 square feet we rent to the Restore Hope Arkansas program.

This inner-city community does not have anything like a Starbucks. So we're about to open up the first coffee shop and a small grocery store because we are in a food desert. We currently have a $4.2 million grant for our nonprofit approved by the State of Arkansas. We're waiting for federal approval. It all comes to the nonprofit, which also then has an aggregate effect, an exponential effect on the church. You can't qualify for a $4.2 million grant from the federal government as a church. So again, structurally, setting up a nonprofit opens up those types of doors and possibilities.

Our mortgage is $16,000 a month, and we receive $13,000 from rental income. That frees up $13,000 every month in tithes and offerings to spend on direct ministry and community impact versus just paying a mortgage to a bank. So, your special teams really help to fund your offense with what I call benevolent ownership.

We learned very quickly that if we're actually going to address needs in a bold and aggressive way, we are going to have to develop multiple streams of income.

Tyrone Barnette

Churches depend on tithes and offerings to support our ministries, and we should. But you've shown us other ways to reach our community and fulfill our mission by leveraging our assets and thinking outside the box.

I know you're helping other churches learn from your experience. Can you talk about that and how others might be able to get involved?

Mark DeYmaz

We conduct a four-and-a-half-month program that is somewhat self-guided and somewhat live coaching with me and my colleague, Dan Davidson. As you know, Tyrone, most pastors lack the experience because nobody teaches you anything about business. Maybe some took a business course, but in the typical general track of a master of divinity degree, you don't get one course on business. In other words, there's an economics to running a church. So we offer something like a mini-MBA-for-pastors crash course. We're helping pastors understand what actual biblical stewardship is.

Nearly 80 percent of giving to the American church is given by people born before 1964. So as older people go away—and I'm one of them at sixty years old—the giving will shift to the younger generations. No, it's not that the younger people won't make money or don't have money. It's that they don't see money and giving the way we do in our generation, because as a group they don't trust institutions. They see volunteerism as equal to giving money. Whereas if you're older, you volunteer in the church, you give money to the church, you tell others about the church.

But the younger you are—if you're born after 1964—it's almost like you pick one of those. I either give money, or I tell people about the church, or I volunteer, but I don't do all three. It's a generational shift in attitudes and approaches to giving that the American church is completely unprepared for. So we teach that.

And then, of course, we teach the functional or practical basics of how to leverage assets to bless the community and ultimately generate some measure of sustainable income to supplement tithes and offerings. We hold you by the hand, and there's homework that you do. You have to come with a couple of people from your church, and together we give you guided instruction and homework that you're doing in between sessions, all to help you identify what you could do that's realistic for you.

Tyrone Barnette

I love what you're doing. I tell you, you are definitely my brother from another mother. And I'm excited about what God is doing and would love to come to Little Rock to see what you're doing firsthand.

17

How Our Young People Can Save the Day

Then Andrew, Simon Peter's brother, spoke up.
"There's a young boy here with five barley loaves and
two fish. But what good is that with this huge crowd?"
JOHN 6:8-9

THE DISCIPLES LOOKED AROUND in the crowd to find food. Only one disciple, Andrew, was able to convince the attendees to offer up their lunch. Surprisingly, it was a young boy who was allowed to contribute. With this one gift, the entire assembly was fed. This young person's meal became the foundation of Christ's miracle. A young person led the way in Jesus' day, and young people can lead the way now—if the adults will give them a chance.

I charge you to look around your congregation and count how many young people are actively engaged in the work of the church, not just those who are coming to church with their parents. How many are actively volunteering and stepping up to assist the mission of the church in some way?

Once you have identified them, attempt to discover what motivates them to serve. What drives them to participate? The answers to those questions may provide us with some of the most important solutions for the church's declining influence on society.

Most would agree that churches are struggling to make vital connections with young people. There is a disconnect on several levels that seems to be growing. One of the most disturbing statistics is the rise of the religiously unaffiliated (the "nones") from less than 10 percent of the United States population in the early 1970s to about 29 percent of adults in 2021.[11] The church is floundering to establish relationships with youth inside our congregations and in the communities. It is past time to discover new ways to build bridges between the generations.

It is the responsibility of leadership to find a way for the youth to feel they belong and are welcomed to contribute to the mission of the church. It requires an earnest desire to see them fully involved at every level of ministry. Teenagers and young adults crave authenticity. Therefore, if the efforts to include them are not sincere, they will sense our patronizing and pull away.

In my experience, the youth are not requiring the older adults to wear skinny jeans, post on Instagram, or create videos on TikTok in order to be relevant and form a relationship. They simply expect their elders to be open to new perspectives and ideas. They want a seat at the table to help guide and inform the church's direction. If we hope to win the world and see lasting change, we will need the youth's energy and insights. Because they see the world in a far different way, they can play an important role as interpreters of culture and navigators for us.

It is important to make a shift in our thinking from "doing ministry" *to* and *for* our youth to serving our communities *along with* our youth. Serving alongside our young people will require a dose of humility and the release of some control to allow them to spread their wings and soar. We must overcome intergenerational tensions and allow Christ-centered unity to bring out the best in everyone.

Tensions arise when older teens and young adults challenge the church's out-of-date and traditional perspectives and practices. Older adults can interpret their questions and objections as rebelliousness and youthful presumption. However, I warn boomers and Gen Xers not to dismiss the millennial and Gen Z cohort as foolhearted and superficial. They may have ways of thinking that can produce the next growth spurt or bold innovation the church needs to take it into the future. The Joshua generation can conquer territory and cross the swollen cultural rivers the previous generations could not overcome. This is especially true as we emerge from this pandemic.

Let's invite them to the table and take full advantage of their skills and expertise. We must be intentional about placing them in positions that match their interests and can move the church forward. They need to be received as full members of the church who have worth and value. They can advise church boards, serve on mission and ministry teams, and lead various initiatives usually reserved for older adults.

At the very least, we can pair them up with seasoned members as apprentices to learn how to lead the ministry later. The apostle Paul invested in younger protégés, such as Timothy and Titus, and encouraged them to take leadership roles in the church. He told Timothy, "Don't let anyone think less of you because you are young. Be an example to all believers in what you say, in the way you live, in your love, your faith, and your purity" (1 Timothy 4:12).

To attract more youth to attend and participate in the life of the church, the church must create an inviting culture that is open to youth. Churches should consider adapting their services to ensure that persons of all ages who are not knowledgeable about Christian phrases, doctrines, and norms are able to gain understanding. No longer can we assume that people are familiar with church lingo and nomenclature. I am not suggesting that we abandon the distinctives that form our faith—I only encourage us to do a better job explaining our language and traditions to a world that has had little exposure.

Reaching young people will revolutionize your church and extend its life for years to come. Too many churches wait too late and resist too long making room for the youth. Jesus said, "Let the children come to me. Don't stop them! For the Kingdom of Heaven belongs to those who are like these children" (Matthew 19:14). The alternative is less promising. Limiting the involvement of youth in the essential life of the church will stabilize it and insulate it from disruption for a time. But soon, the fallacy of barring youth from participation in the decisions and direction of the church will give the church a net zero return on investment in its future.

Use the youth especially to reach your community. They are more aware of what is going on in culture than the average adult. They know the culture's music, movies, and manners. Their connections in schools or colleges and familiarity with social media make them fitting modern-day missionaries. I wouldn't do outreach without the know-how and perception of our youth and young adults. In fact, it would be wise to give them an opportunity to lead and administrate a few mission projects. Support them and provide counsel as they execute their plans. For when you release them to make an impact in an area they are passionate about, they will come alive and you will be amazed at what they can accomplish.

That hillside banquet would not have been the amazing miracle it became without the young lad's lunch. His openhanded benevolence became an inspiration for Christians for centuries. Let's give our youth and young adults full membership in the life and decision-making of the church. They'll be running it soon anyway.

What do the youth in your ministry have to offer? Have you asked them? Are they permitted to play a part in your church's mission? What resistance do they encounter? Once it is discovered, eliminate it.

Jeff Wallace Interview

Jeff currently serves on the Student Leadership University team as the executive director of the LIFT Tour and Youth Pastor Summit. Jeff is nationally known as an urban ministry pioneer, communicator, innovator, and mentor. For twenty-three years, Jeff served as pastor of youth development at Peace Baptist Church in Decatur, Georgia, and then he transitioned to the role of executive pastor. Jeff is also the founder of FrontLine Urban Resources, Inc., an organization that provides resources and training to help leaders engage an evolving generation of families. He is the author of Urban Ministry from Start to Finish *and coauthor of* Everybody's Urban, The Skinny on Communication, *and* 99 Things Every Guy Should Know.

Tyrone Barnette

Tell us a little bit about your role with Student Leadership University.

Jeff Wallace

I started as executive director at Student Leadership University in 2016. We are a Christian parachurch organization that partners with the local church and Christian schools around the world to take students on a leadership journey. We want to give them what we believe is a twenty-year head start on how to develop critical-thinking skills and really understand how to have a biblical worldview—not just how to define their faith, but how to defend it. It's a four-step process, starting in the ninth or tenth grade.

We call the first level 101, and here we take the students to Orlando or San Antonio and teach them the rules, tools, and nuts and bolts of leadership. We're introducing these young people to what it means to be a leader. We believe that leadership is synonymous to discipleship, and we help them maximize their capacity and ability.

The second level is 201. We take the students to Washington, DC, for a week, and they get to hear from a lot of men and women from both the House and the Senate. They'll hear from US Senate Chaplain Barry Black, go to the Press Club, and see all the national monuments. We teach the students leadership principles through the lens of seeing how our government works in the public square.

The next year, for 301, we take them to London, Oxford, Paris, and Normandy. They're going to see and experience leadership through the lens of world history. We talk a lot about Winston Churchill, C. S. Lewis, and John Wesley, and they get a chance to not just *read* about history but walk in it.

And then for 401, the fourth level, we take them to Israel and Jordan. We start with the end in mind because we believe that leadership begins at the feet of Jesus.

I also oversee what we call our front porch ministries or divisions. We have a conference to train youth pastors and their leaders called the Youth Pastor Summit. And then on the LIFT Tours, students go to about twenty different cities and see around twenty thousand students in the spring. So that's the Wikipedia version of what I'm doing now.

Tyrone Barnette

Well, your hands are busy, and what a task you have today! I believe this is the type of training our churches need to be doing with our youth. Our world has changed. And yet the message and mission have to stay the same. How do you think we ought to be reaching young people today? What are you seeing going on in our world?

Jeff Wallace

Well, over the last couple of years, as we've been dealing with the COVID-19 pandemic, we've also seen the polarization of our culture. This generation definitely desires a multicultural approach to church ministry. They want a very diverse and eclectic approach to see equality for the whole man. They want their voices to be heard. And so they're becoming mission oriented. Young people want results right now.

As we are teaching this generation, I think it's important to be Christ-centered and gospel-centered. In other words, preaching the whole counsel of God—which includes everyone. I think they're seeing too much of a single-story perspective of the gospel. And they're not interested in that. They want to see us be more welcoming and less divisive. They want to hear us speaking to issues of today and addressing the real struggles of everyone, and not just one group of people.

Tyrone Barnette

You're seeing this across cultures and ethnicities?

Jeff Wallace

Yes. I think that's the frustration I'm seeing from all White, Black, Latino, Native American, Hispanic, and Asian students.

Tyrone Barnette

Any advice you'd give to a pastor to reach this generation?

Jeff Wallace

I would say don't be afraid to preach and teach on hard things, and on every issue. I'm not saying that pulpits should be polarizing with political rhetoric. That's totally not what I'm saying. I'm saying let's not be afraid to speak about hard things.

Secondly, I think we need to be leveraging digital media. This generation, obviously, is well connected to digital media, in some very creative and innovative ways. I think we can help this generation not lean more toward personal preferences and feelings, but toward biblical truth.

And right now, when things happen in society regarding race, gun violence, and other social issues, there's so much emotion we can't hear each other. I think we are a little bit afraid to engage, because we know that somebody's going to take whatever we say and accuse us of being "too liberal" or we're "too conservative." I think if we stay gospel centered, and we're speaking the truth of the Scriptures, we can never go wrong there. Our young people need us to engage them with the truth.

18

Location, Location, Location

Then Jesus left the vicinity of Tyre and went through Sidon, down
to the Sea of Galilee and into the region of the Decapolis.

MARK 7:31, NIV

THE FEEDING OF THE FIVE THOUSAND is the only one of Christ's
miracles recorded in all four Gospels—with the exception, of
course, of Christ's resurrection. Most people are aware of the
feeding of the five thousand, but few know that Jesus repeated
this miracle with another group sometime later. There are many
compelling differences between these two accounts. One major
difference is the location.

When Jesus fed the five thousand, he was in Jewish territory
near Bethsaida. Luke 9:10 (NIV) records, "When the apostles
returned, they reported to Jesus what they had done. Then he
took them with him and they withdrew by themselves to a town
called Bethsaida." This is where scholars believe the miracle took
place. It is firmly in the Jewish region around the Sea of Galilee.

In contrast, when Jesus performs the miracle of feeding the four thousand, he is in the Gentile region of the ten cities of the Decapolis. Mark writes, "Then Jesus left the vicinity of Tyre and went through Sidon, down to the Sea of Galilee and into the region of the Decapolis" (Mark 7:31, NIV). This region is also known as the region of the Gerasenes.

These are two miracles, at two different times, in two different locations, and with two different ethnic and cultural groups of people. Take note that the miracle of feeding the five thousand occurred in the Jewish district where Jesus and the disciples were familiar, in their own community and among Jews. The second event occurred in the Gentile section of the region in the company of people who were not loyal or especially attentive to Judaism or Jewish culture.

The significance of these events has profound implications for how today's church should operate. Jesus once again teaches us through his actions what it means to be on mission and where and to whom we should direct our efforts. It is no coincidence that Jesus chose to carry out the same miracle with two different groups of people. Even the disciples could not grasp the full magnitude of Christ's wisdom and ingenuity as he skillfully taught a lesson on how the gospel should reach across racial and cultural boundary lines.

He chose to repeat the miraculous feeding in a different area with a vastly distinct people group. Both miracles demonstrate how Jesus can provide and meet needs, but they also encourage us to engage in cross-cultural ministry. The feeding of the four thousand illustrates the importance of taking the gospel outside our comfort zone and places of familiarity, to people and locations that are dissimilar and diverse. As God's chosen people, we are called to do his redemptive work and bring the Bread of Life beyond our neighborhood and throughout the world.

God first gave the commission to Abraham in Genesis 12:1-3 (ESV):

> Now the LORD said to Abram, "Go from your country and your kindred and your father's house to the land that I will show you. And I will make of you a great nation, and I will bless you and make your name great, so that you will be a blessing. I will bless those who bless you, and him who dishonors you I will curse, and in you all the families of the earth shall be blessed."

Christians today are commissioned to take the message to the ends of the earth and to all peoples.

> But you will receive power when the Holy Spirit comes upon you. And you will be my witnesses, telling people about me everywhere—in Jerusalem, throughout Judea, in Samaria, and to the ends of the earth.
> ACTS 1:8

We are meant to be a blessing to everyone and everywhere. Our assignment is to use our energy, time, connections, financial resources, and more to reach people with the gospel. It is often convenient to stay in our protected and homogeneous circles. We prefer to be in familiar places and around people who look like, talk like, eat like, and think like us. But God's Spirit is always pushing us toward the borders beyond our familiar Jerusalem, toward Samaria, where all nine characteristics of the fruit of the Spirit will be examined for their ripeness.

An example of a modern-day Samaria is a place or people that are geographically close to you but culturally, racially, or economically far. Are there people or places in your city or town that you sense God is calling you to have some impact on? How should you be preparing yourself to go?

PART II

PRACTICAL OUTREACH TO YOUR COMMUNITY

19

Outreach Ideas
for the Local Church

MANY PEOPLE IN CHURCHES have a predetermined picture of what outreach and community ministry are supposed to be. Some take the approach of planting a new church in a new community that is different from the mother church. Others seek to start a church-based nonprofit entity and run several programs from it, while other churches launch new initiatives from within the already existing programs and assign various aspects of outreach to different departments or staff. Several churches will partner with other ministries or community groups and send money or volunteers to support that organization.

There are myriad ways a church can get involved in outreach. There is no one perfect way that a church can fulfill its Great Commission calling. The particular pathway and configuration of how community ministry is carried out will depend on the gifts, abilities, passions, needs, opportunities, and resources a congregation possesses.

The hope is that the church will find a way that is beneficial to the community and that meets spiritual, relational, economic, educational, and social needs. And at the same time, the work should also be rewarding to the congregation so that members' gifts are used and developed and the church is viewed as an essential part of that community.

Striking a balance is the responsibility of the church's senior leadership. There is a possibility that a ministry objective may be beneficial to the community but not advantageous to the church. Or a project can be good for the church but injurious to the community. For instance, a church could launch an outreach project that requires an overwhelming number of volunteers, resources, and follow-up. The congregation could start with zeal and commitment but later become overwhelmed by the ongoing responsibility and demands of the ministry, causing volunteers to drop out and resources to dry up. What began with great enthusiasm soon fizzles into poorly designed and ineffective ministry initiatives that hurt the witness of the church in the community.

Churches are prone to overcommit and underestimate the cost of carrying out ministry for the long haul. One-day events often make the church feel good about their efforts, but without an ongoing plan to effect lasting change, the community is often left feeling used, dropped, and abandoned when there is no long-term vision beyond the one-day event.

It is better to be consistent in outreach efforts to a community by providing ongoing ministry so that relationships can be formed and trust established between the residents and the church. By listening and forming relationships within the community, the church will discover what the true needs are and unearth gifts and abilities within the residents. In this way, a true partnership can be formed that will not damage the community but help it to discover its dreams and reach its maximum potential.

Over the years, our church has launched many outreach programs. The ones that have been successful are the programs for which we took time to invest in training for the volunteers, when we spent time in the community listening to its leaders and allowing them to tell us what they needed, and when we maintained a commitment to stay engaged for an extended period of time.

Ministry is hard, and doing ministry within the community context is even harder. Each church must make some decisions on how it will develop and carry out its outreach strategy. My encouragement is to be flexible and do not be afraid of trying different tactics and methods to achieve your objective. Be willing to admit when you have made a mistake or bit off more than you can chew.

Yet be open to the exciting new doors God will present to you. Each new venture will stretch you, and the new relationships you will form will force you to apply the Scriptures and exercise your faith in ways that will widen your worldview and understanding of others. You will be tempted to stay within your own cultural context and play it safe to reach out to people who look like, think like, and act like you do. However, the grand adventure God has in store for you is found in investigating and intentionally participating in cross-cultural ministry.

In the story of Jesus and the Samaritan woman, John records that Jesus "had to go through Samaria" on his way from Judea to Galilee.[12] I believe this is not only a reference to the fact that it was geographically closer to walk through Samaria, but also to the fact that Jesus' mission compelled and obligated him to go through Samaria. In other words, he purposely took his ministry through that region and spoke to a woman who was different from him in race, gender, culture, worship, and lifestyle. He *had* to go through Samaria.

Later, John 4:27 (NIV) reads, "Just then his disciples returned and were surprised to find him talking with a woman. But no one asked, 'What do you want?' or 'Why are you talking with her?'"

His disciples were surprised Jesus was engaging in a conversation with a Samaritan woman. Jewish men did not fellowship with Samaritans, especially women, and few even walked through that region. But God calls us to Samaria. Samaria is that place that is close to you or your church in proximity but far from you culturally. Geographically, it's close to you, but it's far from you racially, economically, socially, politically, and in a myriad of ways. Nevertheless, God calls us to go through Samaria, to step within its borders, and to do our best to make an impact.

Jesus had to go through Samaria. Where or to whom do you have to go to fulfill your calling? What people group or territory must your church attempt to reach that is outside your comfort zone? What new ministry initiatives is God calling you to establish?

In the following section, I will offer a few practical suggestions on how to make the necessary shifts and reorganize your church and volunteers to reach your community and transform your Samaria. Perhaps God is calling you or your church to start a new ministry or to renovate an existing one. Maybe it's time to create a nonprofit ministry or form a partnership with another ministry or organization. I hope these remaining chapters will offer you some invaluable insight.

20

Create a Church-Sponsored 501(c)(3)

ONE NIGHT I WAS AWAKENED from a dream in which our church was the center of the community. I could see it from an elevated bird's-eye view as I looked down on the building. I could see through the roof and witness the activity going on inside. I saw hundreds of people coming to our building and standing in two lines. One line led into the sanctuary, where those who came in could experience the worship service. The other line of people entered a separate section to get food, clothes, and talk with someone at what looked like a help desk at a hospital or office building.

The group who passed through the worship center walked by the pulpit and continued to the other side of the building where the second group entered. As they went, they passed those who had received clothes and food as they moved toward the sanctuary for worship. In short, each group experienced worship and received some sort of assistance from the church to meet their everyday needs.

I told my wife and a few leaders about my dream. I shared that I believed God was calling us to launch a community development corporation or a nonprofit of some kind. This new entity would allow us to reach people who were not initially coming to the church to worship but had some personal or family issue we could address. And by building relationships with them, my hope was that they would see the love of Christ in us and decide to follow him.

After hearing this idea, a few leaders wondered why we needed to start a new organization. We already had a vibrant food ministry, clothing closet, recovery program, a foster care program, and an adult educational ministry helping people obtain GEDs and work/life skills. They believed that forming a nonprofit would create a level of complexity that was unnecessary. Additionally, there was a concern that the cost of starting another corporation, combined with our lack of experience, might distract us from our mission.

So I brought in a consultant who had a good track record for helping churches successfully establish nonprofits. He shared with us the benefits and challenges of forming a separate 501(c)(3), and his counsel helped to relieve most of the concerns. Once members understood that the nonprofit would exist to support the missional purposes of the church, they were 100 percent on board, and within six months Peace on the Move, Inc. was born. It now serves as an autonomous intermediary organization aligned with the missional focus of the church. It operates with a separate board and budget to create and administer outreach programs in our area. For over twenty years, Peace on the Move, Inc. has served as an invaluable partner in our efforts to transform our community. As a separate entity, it has been able to secure funding and support that would not have been possible through the church.

Perhaps your church is ready to set up a nonprofit community development corporation (CDC) to operate a school, a health clinic, a program to reach at-risk youth, job training, a senior day-care center, or a plethora of other community ministry ventures. Once an outreach or community-based program in your church develops a level of complexity as it grows and expands, it may be time to consider placing it within a separate nonprofit structure. When these types of programs grow, they tend to require a lot more of the church staff's and governing board's time and can become a strain on finances if all their funding is dependent on the church's tithes and offerings. Creating a 501(c)(3) could help to alleviate that pressure and cause both organizations to thrive.

In this way, the church can focus on its work without having to manage all the operations of the 501(c)(3), and the nonprofit can be laser-focused on its work and responsibilities. I've noticed that CDCs can often move quicker and take advantage of opportunities more readily than a church that has a more intricate and elaborate decision-making process. Sometimes grant applications open and close with very short deadlines. And some churches miss out because their administrative schedule is slower than a narrowly focused 501(c)(3).

Also, your church may consider forming a separate 501(c)(3) if the policies and structure of the church place limits on what the nonprofit can do and how it can function. For instance, a CDC may need more space than the church can provide and may have to move to expand its operations. Perhaps there is the need to access volunteers outside the church membership.

We have been able to partner with many corporations and businesses that want to send volunteers to work in our programs, but their policies forbid them to send employees to a church. However, they are happy to assist with our church's nonprofit. As a result, we have more than one hundred volunteers on our campus working with Peace on the Move, Inc. annually. Our members work alongside these corporate volunteers, and we have seen many lives changed in this collaboration of the secular and sacred.

The chief reason for churches to form community development corporations is the church's need to attract outside funding from Christian and secular groups that place restrictions on contributing to a church directly. Typically, there are fewer constraints on giving to a 501(c)(3) than to a church. Plus, it's a good idea to segregate the church's funding and financial records from those of the nonprofit, because it is a more efficient way to organize the required annual reporting and audit process. This separation will also be important when the nonprofit applies for grants. They have a better chance of being awarded some grants if they can provide financial statements that are independent of the church's.

Another reason for creating a community development corporation is that it allows the 501(c)(3) to assemble a board from inside and outside the church's membership to provide the necessary executive and philanthropic competencies. Most church boards have godly men and women who serve on them, but they may lack the management expertise to administer the nonprofit entity. Church board members may be proficient in matters related to Scripture and church culture. However, a special skill set is essential for handling grant funds and endowments, and for the strict documentation and detail that grants require to be filled out periodically.

Making the choice to launch a new, separate corporation has some built-in risks. As already mentioned, it will require a separate board made up of church members but may also include persons who are not members. Some of the grant funding sources want to see that your board includes representation of people within the community who are not affiliated with your church. You have to decide if this stipulation is something you would adhere to. If not, then look for other sources that do not impose this condition. If you do bring someone on board who is not a member, do your due diligence by confirming that they are in line with the beliefs and values of the church. You will be giving a lot of influence and authority to a board member who could potentially derail your mission.

There is always the possibility that by creating a separate autonomous organization the nonprofit can wander away from its faith-focused mission, especially if it is not set up to be closely associated and allied with the church. Secular groups that financially support it could compel the nonprofit to shy away from a spiritual emphasis that could limit the gospel's influence on the people it serves. For us, we have decided not to pursue any resources or opportunities that restrict us from our number one goal of making Christ known.

There are, unfortunately, hundreds of examples of Christian-based ministries that started out with a strong faith focus, and because they received secular or governmental subsidies, they were forced to remove all references to religion. One church started an impressive drug recovery program for women that included daily Bible study, mandated discipleship activities, and prayer. As they expanded, they received a large grant from an organization that required them to eliminate all mentions of faith unless the client brought it up. This constraint radically changed the nature of the program and hindered the ability of women to experience a true breakthrough from addiction. Once the leaders decided to stop receiving the secular funding and reinstated the spiritual principles that were the original core of their program, the women began to experience lasting transformation once again.

This possible faith drift is the most dangerous obstacle the church may face when establishing a community development corporation. Therefore, I am going to beat the drum once again on this important detail. To guard against a faith or mission drift, ensure that if the nonprofit's board includes anyone from outside the church, they understand and agree with the church's core values and scriptural beliefs.

We have decided only to invite professing Christians with a Great Commission mindset on our boards. We also make sure that our nonprofit's board has a majority of church members on it, along with me as pastor, serving as an ex officio (nonvoting) member of the board. This arrangement keeps the church and nonprofit in sync. Annually, I share the vision of the church and give a charge to the nonprofit board that is in line with our joint overall mission. In addition to going to occasional meetings with the board, I am copied on all the activities and decisions the board makes, and I maintain a very close working relationship with the board chair and officers.

To further avoid a faith drift in our nonprofit corporation, we only partner with secular or governmental groups that respect our faith-based approach to outreach. Over the years we have received hundreds of thousands of dollars from faith-based and non-faith-based organizations. We decided years ago that we would fund our ministries from the faithful tithes and offerings of our members but would not restrict funding opportunities from other organizations that coincided with our goals and objectives.

I was greatly influenced by Rick Rusaw and Eric Swanson's 2004 publication of *The Externally Focused Church*. They offer a balanced approach to working with and receiving assistance from secular organizations. They write, "Although some churches question the advisability of partnering with secular organizations, remember the criteria: *they are* morally positive (they are doing good things) and spiritually neutral (they don't have a spiritual agenda of their own)."[13]

This qualifier has been a guiding principle for us and led us to partner with United Way, the U.S. Department of Education, our public school system, the county court system, police departments, food banks, the county family and children services department, drug rehabilitation centers, and dozens of other organizations that are morally positive and spiritually neutral. Some are open to work with the church directly, while others prefer to work through our nonprofit.

Either way, the church and the nonprofit need to ensure they manage the resources and volunteers of the secular organization with excellence. It is a powerful witness to agencies and their employees of what a mutually beneficial partnership can produce as they work together to address societal needs. Therefore, it is important to have first-rate processes and administrative fidelity when managing the resources of your organization. The secular world needs to know that faith-based organizations will properly handle resources and operate efficiently.

We have been able to open opportunities for many faith-based groups to work with secular charities and governmental agencies that were closed to churches and faith-based organizations in the past. We demonstrated that our church or 501(c)(3) could get paperwork filled out correctly, pass stringent financial audits, and meet our stated goals within the allotted time limits of the grant. Many times our local government or other secular organizations will reach out to us and give us resources without asking because they trust we will handle the resources and provide quality care to the people we assist.

When forming a 501(c)(3), the church must determine how the new nonprofit will be structured and what programs it will include. Some churches create one community development corporation that encompasses all the church's outreach programs, while others form separate 501(c)(3) organizations for each ministry objective. I know of one church in Houston that has over ten separate organizations. However, that means ten separate boards, ten separate budgets and operational processes. Most churches are not able to manage a complicated structure with so many moving parts. The best and simplest method is to have one 501(c)(3) with one board that oversees various programs.

Forming a separate community development corporation is not for every church. And no church should start one just to receive extra funding. The motive should be to have a greater capacity to spread the gospel in your community and beyond. It is equally important that you make an effort to ensure the nonprofit stays visible to the congregation and that they are aware of its programs and the challenges and successes it encounters. The congregation should never assume that outside funders and outside volunteers are responsible the nonprofit's programs. There is a danger that the congregation may feel they have no obligation to the mission work of the 501(c)(3) and choose not to participate in or contribute resources to its programs. Therefore, make an intentional effort to keep the church intertwined and connected to the work of the nonprofit through special programs, an annual giving emphasis, church publications, the church's website, frequent public testimonies of transformation, and by mentioning it often in sermons and illustrations from the pulpit.

One final word of caution when reaching the community with the gospel in the church and through the 501(c)(3). While we are careful not to employ aggressive and overassertive evangelistic tactics in our community-based programs, we do zealously seek to build relationships with everyone we serve. No one must be a Christian or hold any particular belief or creed for us to serve them. All our programs are open to anyone, and no one is denied assistance based on any criteria. For we have decided that lifestyle evangelism is the best means to share our faith and influence others to adopt a Christian way of life. Many of the people we serve find Christ and experience life change without ever hearing a sermon. The blinding light of love and hospitality on display from our members who serve our community preaches louder and more eloquently than a year's worth of Sunday messages.

21

Empty Pockets, Full Hearts: Establishing a Donation Ministry

I THINK MY FAVORITE CHURCHES in the Bible are the Macedonian churches. Philippi, Thessalonica, and Berea specifically are often grouped together by theologians. They were a heavily persecuted collection of churches in northern Greece. Paul writes in 2 Corinthians 8:1-4:

> Now I want you to know, dear brothers and sisters, what God in his kindness has done through the churches in Macedonia. They are being tested by many troubles, and they are very poor. But they are also filled with abundant joy, which has overflowed in rich generosity. For I can testify that they gave not only what they could afford, but far more. And they did it of their own free will. They

begged us again and again for the privilege of sharing in
the gift for the believers in Jerusalem.

These were some of the poorest and most persecuted churches
during Paul's time. One would think that they would be bitter and
disconnected from the work of God, focusing on their own needs.
Yet, this band of oppressed and destitute believers were some of the
most generous and giving Christians in the New Testament. They are
characterized as having nothing, but they found a way to give despite
their disadvantages. Paul says they pleaded with him to give them an
opportunity to raise an offering for the suffering saints in Jerusalem.

The Macedonians would not allow their charitable spirit to be
drowned out by a tidal wave of dreadful circumstances or horrific
deprivation. They found a way to share what little they had as
they were moved by the stories of suffering experienced by their
brethren thousands of miles away in Jerusalem. They chose to not
sit idly by and do nothing. So they reached below their own pov-
erty line and found a way to share with others. The Macedonian
churches are a model of ministry for us today and stand as a gentle
rebuke and forceful reminder that every church and Christian
needs to follow their example.

When churches are looking for a way to have a positive impact
on their communities, the simplest and most immediate way to
start is to launch a donation ministry. In this model, the church
collects donations of many kinds to distribute to the community
or for a specific people group in need. We are all familiar with
church food pantries and have more than likely asked members
to bring in canned goods or nonperishables to distribute when
someone comes asking for food. Or perhaps you have collected
socks to give out to the homeless, or school supplies for kids in
the neighboring schools.

A well-designed donation ministry is an uncomplicated and straightforward way for members to get involved. It doesn't require a lot of time, it doesn't require a lot of personal interaction, and those who donate can remain relatively anonymous. Additionally, it doesn't cost much to set up. A church of any size, with very few volunteers, can begin one.

One other benefit is that it can be used to draw attention to serious needs in the church's community or around the world. For instance, a request to the congregation for food or clothing for the homeless population in the area could bring attention to their plight and living conditions. Many who attend church every week may not even notice the presence of homeless men, women, and children who are barely surviving in the shadows of the church. During the collection drive, the church can become educated and learn about how mental illness, the lack of health care, and post-traumatic stress disorder affect military veterans, who may make up a large part of the homeless community in the area. Or the church may become knowledgeable about the education deficiency of children who are innocent victims of homelessness and decide to establish a new ministry to address their specialized needs.

My hope is that churches that employ this donation model would pair it with other programs or services they provide, or at least refer those they serve to another church or agency in the community to address the deeper need. We are always looking for ways to link our donation and charitable distribution events to either a spiritual, educational, relational, vocational, or recovery program. A donation model shouldn't just be a Band-Aid to cover up the real bleeding wound that led the persons you serve to be in need in the first place. Ultimately, we know the real need is spiritual, but in most cases, we have to attend to the physical, financial, or emotional problem that gave rise to the problem initially.

While it is true that a donation ministry is a vital outreach program that is most likely present in some form in every church, it does have its disadvantages. One such challenge to be avoided is not to create a donation model that makes the people served dependent on the organization. We certainly want to address needs, but we do not want to create an unhealthy dependence on the church.

Robert Lupton shares a stark warning in *Toxic Charity*: "Relationships built on need are seldom healthy. . . . Relationships built on need tend to be short-lived. . . . Relationships built on need do not reduce need. Rather, they require more and more to continue."[14]

Other considerations include determining whether the members are financially in a position to go out and purchase the desired items. If the congregation is made up of a large number of unemployed or financially disadvantaged persons, be sure to request items they can afford, or design a way for them to partner with others to purchase a higher priced item as a team.

You also want to ensure that you do not have a donation model that limits interaction between the recipients of the services and the congregation. When congregants donate goods by just dropping off an item at the church or placing it in a bin in the lobby, it doesn't connect them to the lives of the people in need.

Take the donation model to another level and think of ways that the congregation can interact with the people you serve. Link your food distribution or Christmas giveaway to some planned community event so that relationships can form. Continue to donate items to the local public schools in your area, but don't just deliver the items to the loading dock. Give out the school supplies at a sporting event, PTA meeting, teacher-parent conference night, or at some other school activity so that your church members can intermingle with the community.

Perhaps the most common shortcoming of a donation model is that members may bring items that are in poor condition. The church donation model should not be an opportunity for members to unload their unwanted goods on the church. Old and worn merchandise should not be accepted and distributed to those in need. Insist on quality goods to be given as a proper witness to God and of your church. Food items should be what members would eat themselves and not out-of-date. When people are impoverished and in desperate need, we must always seek to maintain their dignity and serve them with respect. Therefore, whatever is distributed should be new or nearly new to reflect the excellence of our Lord and to honor the self-worth of the recipient.

Make sure you have storage space for the items and a proper place to distribute them. It is wise to have certain designated times when you give out what you've collected. Post service times when the ministry operates so that people come when you are equipped to serve. Be careful of donating money to people and have strict guidelines for when you do. I suggest you create one policy for members and another for the community.

One example at our church is the Sonshine Nursing Home Ministry. It serves ten nursing and convalescent homes in our community. One team of members conducts one-hour worship services, either weekly or monthly at each site, and develops ongoing relationships with the residents, staff, and their families. Over forty clergy and nonclergy members work together to produce this service with singing, preaching, and various forms of fellowship at each gathering.

Because not everyone in our church feels comfortable or called to sing or teach a lesson before a room full of strangers, the leaders wanted to find a way to involve the entire church in what they do and keep the ministry before the congregation on an ongoing basis. So several times a year, usually centered around a holiday, we ask the church to donate different items to give to the over four hundred residents in the centers. One season we collect brand-new soft throw blankets, at another time we ask for brand-new robes, or we request members to fill and decorate a shoe box with toiletries. Everyone in the church gets involved, and we are able to share the love of Christ with many of them who rarely receive anything from family or friends.

Is there an existing ministry or program in your church that could benefit from this type of infusion of resources to enhance what they already do?

Any church can launch a donation ministry. The Macedonians were as poor as church mice, but they found a way to give despite their personal or corporate hardship. It is even more important today for the church to be engaged in meeting the temporal needs of our communities. As a church gives, the Lord provides greater opportunities to reach the community and provides even more abundant resources to the church and its members. Giving in this way leads to a spirit of generosity throughout the church, and the community views the church as an essential ally in the neighborhood.

22

Building a House of Prayer: The Power That Fuels Your Outreach

NOTHING OF TRUE ETERNAL SIGNIFICANCE happens in God's Kingdom without prayer undergirding our efforts. The power of our evangelistic endeavors will not be the quality or innovations of our programs. Nor will it be due to the high-capacity leaders who matriculated from our finest and best seminaries.

At the core of every Christ-centered and community-focused program strategy there must be the dominant presence of prayer that empowers the leadership, arranges the opportunities, and opens the hearts of people to receive the gospel of Jesus. Every church that I have witnessed do an effective job in community outreach has made prayer a priority. The power of the Holy Spirit must be present if we ever hope to win our communities for the Lord. A church's potent prayer ministry with a focus on evangelism will break up the hard soil of its neighborhood and make it fertile ground for an abundant harvest of souls.

Sadly, if the Holy Spirit left many churches today, it would be weeks or months before anyone noticed. We rely so much on human effort and our own ingenuity and rarely depend on the Spirit's leading, inspiration, and empowerment. Second Timothy 3:5 (NIV) might be said about the American church: "Having a form of godliness but denying its power."

Do not overlook or take for granted the first part of the statement of Jesus in Acts 1:8, which reads, "But you will receive power when the Holy Spirit comes upon you. And you will be my witnesses, telling people about me everywhere—in Jerusalem, throughout Judea, in Samaria, and to the ends of the earth."

Jesus does not send us out to reach the four corners of the world without the power of the Holy Spirit. Without his enablement, we would wear out under the colossal weight of pain, disruption, and sin in our own local Jerusalem. We would never make it to Judea or Samaria, and we would by no means reach the world. Perhaps the reason Christians are declining in influence today is because we did not call on and depend on the power of the Holy Spirit yesterday. Maybe we should not attempt to launch anything new in our churches until we have followed the command of Jesus to wait for the empowerment of God's Spirit (Acts 1:4).

When the first-century believers were being terrorized and bullied by their oppressors, they cried out to God for assistance. They prayed, "And now, O Lord, hear their threats, and give us, your servants, great boldness in preaching your word. Stretch out your hand with healing power; may miraculous signs and wonders be done through the name of your holy servant Jesus" (Acts 4:29-30).

They prayed that God would give them unusual boldness to witness during tremendous persecution and opposition. They appealed to God to give them power to perform miraculous wonders in the name of Jesus. After their prayer, the meeting room shook, and the believers were galvanized to preach and reach their community with the life-giving remedy of the gospel (Acts 4:31).

This does not have to be something we just read about in the sacred pages of our Bibles. We can each experience the groundbreaking potential of the gospel if we would dare cry out to God individually and corporately. We, too, can observe miracles and wonders as God uses us to change our neighborhood and make it safe for everyone. We can be used to bring life back into the local school in our community through some God-inspired vision he gives us for the students and teachers. By working together with other like-minded believers, we can restore families, give hope to the marginalized, and change the condition for hundreds and thousands of people around our church and throughout the world. Prayer will be the key that unlocks the door to each of these wonders.

Turning Your Church into a House of Prayer

First, prayer is more caught than taught. In other words, you learn to pray by doing it and not just planning to pray. As one of my mentors always says, "Stop talking about it and be about it." As you develop principles for the prayer ministry, it may look different from church to church. But there are some general characteristics that will be in any prayer ministry. The first is the need for pastoral support.

A fervent prayer ministry begins with the support of the pastor and leadership. In most churches, no one has more influence than the pastor. Getting him on board will be essential for it to disseminate through the whole church. I've never met a pastor who turned away someone who was earnest about prayer and wanted to inspire the church to pray. The only exception has been when the person has an agenda that does not line up with the church's vision or if the person is attempting to build a ministry program around themselves. Most pastors can easily discern those persons and will be cautious in giving them too much latitude.

If you are approaching your pastor about starting or relaunching a prayer ministry, be humble and sincere. Ask the pastor what his dream is for an effective prayer ministry and assist him in bringing that vision to light. However, be ready to suggest a path forward if the pastor does not have clear direction and gives you freedom to proceed. Keep him informed as you progress. The pastor should delegate the administrative and decision-making aspects of the prayer ministry to the team, but he should never delegate the vision.

Secondly, there should be a commitment to be consistent in prayer. As Paul says in Colossians 4:2, "Devote yourselves to prayer with an alert mind and a thankful heart."

The prayer ministry should not be just another program in the church. Nor should a church settle for just praying together when they gather for worship and check the box that prayer has been done. The prayer ministry should be that ministry that undergirds all other ministries. It is the foundational one that keeps everything moving.

I remember hearing a story that Charles Spurgeon had a visit from a group of ministers who wanted to know the reason for his church's success and effectiveness in reaching people. Spurgeon shared that it was the "boiler room" that kept the church on fire.[15] The visitors wanted to visit the boiler room. He took them to the basement and opened the door to dozens of members who gathered there every day in shifts to pray for the church, its pastor, and the community. Every church needs a "boiler room of prayer" that keeps the church aflame.

For years we have had a weekly, early morning prayer call for thirty to sixty minutes. But at the beginning of the pandemic our excellent prayer leader asked if we could extend it to every day of the week. We thought we would just do it for a few weeks and go back to our regular weekly schedule. However, it was so well received by the membership that it grew beyond any numbers we had previously recorded. For the past three years on any given day, seventy-five to one hundred fifty or more are on the call every morning at 6:00. I credit this modern day "boiler room" as the reason our church has thrived and remained focused on the mission of reaching the world for Christ. You do not need to gather daily as we do, or have people praying around the clock like Spurgeon, but there needs to be a consistent cadence of prayer for your church.

Thirdly, a church needs a prayer coordinator who is surrendered to God, already possesses an enriching personal prayer life, and is willing to be accountable to God, the pastor, and the congregation. Furthermore, they need to be supportive of the church's vision and able to recruit others to join the prayer ministry team. No one person can do this alone.

One suggestion is to recruit team members from every major ministry in the church to simultaneously serve on the prayer team. This will allow for the prayer ministry to have representation from all areas of the church. Their role will be to bring to the collective prayer team the needs of the specific ministry or department and intercede for its members. Have the leader of a given ministry appoint someone to work with the prayer coordinator. This simple step will unify the church dramatically as you raise up prayer warriors throughout the congregation. This team should meet quarterly for prayer and strategy planning.

The fourth principle is to develop a prayer strategy for the entire church. Now that there is a prayer leader in every ministry—children, students, adult education, administration, worship, first impressions (greeters/ushers), outreach, men's and women's ministries, singles, senior adults, outreach, etc.—the prayer ministry advances a plan. The plan could be twofold: one prayer strategy for a specific or departmental ministry created by the prayer leader assigned to it, and an overall churchwide strategy to involve everyone in the church.

The churchwide strategy should include an inward and outward focus. Here are some ideas of inward-focused prayer initiatives for your church:

- Arrange for periodic prayer training, workshops, and courses for the members.
- Create an intercessory prayer room in the church or wall of prayer in the lobby.
- Collect and pray through the prayer cards that come in after the weekly worship services.
- Conduct periodic corporate prayer meetings and services (National Day of Prayer, prayer breakfast events, etc.).
- Organize prayer retreats.
- Coordinate prayer partners among the members.
- Schedule other activities that are primarily for members.

The outward-focused prayer ministry centers on the community, both local and global.

- At every community event, such as a block party, outdoor fall festival, or community food distribution, ensure that the prayer ministry is visible to all who attend.

- If you have a mobile food ministry where clients stay in their cars waiting to be served, have prayer team members go by each car and offer to pray with them.
- Have the prayer team go to grocery stores and malls with a prayer tent and offer to pray with people.
- Give the prayer team the responsibility to keep foreign missionaries and local community needs before the church.
- Allow the prayer team to lead the church in corporate prayer on Sundays from time to time.
- Arrange for prayer walks or prayer drives around the community to assess needs and to stay attentive and responsive to changes that are occurring in the neighborhood.
- Join with other local churches and conduct a concert of prayer event for your area, where you invite politicians and other leaders to come and be prayed for by the Christian community.

It will take intercessory prayer to reach our community and see true transformation. Actually, we should not just pray for missions, but see prayer *as* the mission. When we begin to pray for our communities, we have already begun to reach them. Prayer prepares the soil for the seed of the Word to be planted in the hearts of those we encounter and empowers those who will be sent to spread the seed and collect the harvest. Nothing significant will happen without prayer.

23

Creating a Ministry Plan

FOR THE PAST THIRTY YEARS, I've served as the pastor of one church. I've watched it grow from a few members to thousands in that time span. Pastors ask me, What is one practical thing a church can do to keep its ministry growing and unified over the long haul? My answer is always to encourage them to make sure every ministry in their church operates with a ministry plan.

A ministry plan does more than describe what a ministry or department does. It describes how it operates, communicates, and is structured. It forecasts goals, clarifies the values, and explains how members are recruited and leaders trained. It becomes an operational guide that is aligned with the vision and mission of the church.

Many years ago, we met with a church consultant who forced us to take a hard look at how our church was structured and operating. At our first meeting he gave us a short assessment to evaluate how we were managing our ministry. Take this simple assessment by answering true or false for one specific program or department in your church. Since this book is about outreach, pick something from that ministry area. However, you could apply this assessment to any ministry in your church.

	True	False
1. If the primary leader of the ministry area quit today, the new leader would have a written document of how the ministry operates.		
2. The positions and tasks of each person in the ministry area are well-defined and understood by each person involved in this area.		
3. The congregation operates with a written description of each program and/or activity that is offered by the ministry.		
4. The ministry area works from a set of annual goals and objectives that are assessed regularly.		
5. Everyone involved in the ministry area has a working knowledge of the budget for the ministry area.		
6. Everyone in the ministry has a working knowledge of the policies and procedures that make the ministry work.		
7. There is a master calendar of events, activities, and meetings for the current year.		
8. The ministry has a clearly defined marketing, advertising, and promotional plan for the year.		
9. The church staff has access to a written plan of your facilities and equipment plan for the year.		
10. A formal leadership training course is currently in place for anyone who becomes involved in the ministry.		
TOTAL SCORE		

If you have seven or more false answers, it may be time for you to consider a reorganization plan for your church and the specific ministries under each department. After meeting with our consultant and applying his advice, we began to structure many areas of our church in a way that boosted morale, unified the entire church, and created a season of sustained health that continues to this day.

What follows are some principles we developed, applying insights from our consultation, to help us structure most of the ministries in our church. For over twenty years we have treasured these processes and have seen much fruit come from them. I trust they will guide you as well.

First, I suggest you form a ministry development team that is made up of key leaders from the various departments of your church and have them apply these processes to their specific ministries. Further, if there have been discussions about starting a new ministry or initiative, these recommendations will help to provide some structure.

Pastors are often approached by members or leaders to start new ministries. When people come to me with an idea to launch some new program, I have them answer most of these questions. It helps me see that they have a clearly defined plan to proceed and gives me invaluable insight in their ability to lead and administrate the program if it is enacted.

Organizing most of your church's programs and ministries with this same administrative structure promotes unity and creates a common language that permeates the church.

Outline of a Ministry Plan

1. Purpose

a. Develop a one- or two-sentence statement that defines this ministry's purpose.

b. Write a one- or two-paragraph statement that describes what this ministry will look like in three years. Who is the target group it will reach? What will be the results of the ministry? How will you achieve these results?

c. List the core values of this ministry area.

d. What are your expectations for everyone working in this ministry area?

e. List a few Scriptures that support or describe this ministry area.

2. Personnel

a. Create an organizational chart of the leadership structure. Do not just draw what you have currently but include every position you will need in the future to be fully functional.

b. Write out a job description for each position on the chart, paid and volunteer. List the purpose of the position, the time involved in serving, the tasks involved, the qualifications for the role, and the resources needed to do the job.

c. Describe how leaders and volunteers will be recruited.

d. Describe what training will be needed for the ministry leaders and volunteers. What curriculum will you use?

e. Determine when and how often the training will be offered.

f. Describe how you will evaluate the leaders and ministry at least biannually or annually. Who will evaluate them?

g. How will you encourage and motivate the leaders and volunteers throughout the year?

3. Projections, Goals, and Objectives

a. Define the goals and objectives for the overall ministry.

4. Programs and Events

a. Plan each major program, activity, ministry, and event that will be the responsibility of this ministry.

b. Develop a planning timeline for each event. What will be the follow-up plan after the event? How will you record attendance, decisions made, and other important statistics and outcomes?

5. Property Schedule

a. For each activity or event, schedule the event on the church calendar and schedule the facility and equipment needed for the event.

6. Promotions and Marketing

a. For each activity or event, develop a promotions and marketing plan.

b. How will you inform the church or community about your event?

c. What means of communication will you use to advertise the event?

d. How will you use church announcements, publications, social media, the church website, community newspapers, etc.?

e. Who is the target group the promotion is aiming for?

f. How will you keep the ministry before the congregation and share with them the needs, successes, and challenges of the ministry area?

g. In your marketing, have a compelling reason people should attend your event. How will the event or ministry benefit attendees?

7. Purchases/Budget

a. For each activity or event, develop a projected budget. Compile an overall twelve-month budget for the ministry.

The value of organizing most of your church's programs and ministries with this same administrative structure promotes unity and creates a common language that permeates the church. Persons outside the church should be able to read the formulated plans for the ministry and get a clear picture of how it operates, the capacity of its leaders, and the expected outcomes. It also aids senior leadership in planning and provides them with a tool for evaluating the church's ministries. One other benefit is that this process will reduce incidences of hastily devised plans that often generate frustration and do not produce the best the church can offer.

I encourage you to look at your current programs, especially those that reach out to the community, and consider whether they are structured in ways that are giving you the results you desire. These documents will allow the ministry or program not to suffer if a key leader leaves or resigns. If that happens, all the important information is in writing for the next leaders to follow. It will take some energy and an investment of time, but the subsequent advantages will serve your church and community well for years to come if you implement this approach.

24

Outreach Ideas
Any Church Can Do

CONGREGATIONS OF ANY SIZE can do a variety of projects to reach their community. Without a lot of resources or volunteers, significant inroads can be made to meet people's needs. Many ideas don't require a lot of skill to be successful. What's needed is people who are willing to listen and open to being used by God as conduits of his grace.

As you encounter people, look for opportunities to share the gospel without pressure. Sometimes we are so excited about the prospect of leading someone to the Lord that we attempt to force something to happen. The people you will come across may not even know that they need a relationship with Christ. So be patient and allow the Spirit of God to lead you. You may have to have several encounters before the people you serve are even ready to have a conversation about faith.

Paul writes in 1 Corinthians 3:6, "I planted the seed in your hearts, and Apollos watered it, but it was God who made it grow." Be aware of the importance of each step throughout the entire redemptive process and be content with whatever role the Spirit has assigned for you to play.

When you implement your missional tasks, a few things may go wrong. No matter how much you plan and anticipate challenges, there will be something you didn't consider that will threaten to derail your best efforts. Don't get discouraged, but be exceedingly flexible and ready to pivot when obstacles arise—whether it's an unexpected thunderstorm, a hostile neighbor, funding that doesn't come through at the last minute, or one of a thousand other mishaps that can upset even the best-laid plans. Remember that we serve a sovereign God who is never taken by surprise. He has a way of using misfortune to demonstrate to us that without him we can do nothing, and as Gideon discovered, he alone will receive the glory (Judges 7:1-22).

Just stay organized, because if you are not, disorder and confusing processes will discourage and frustrate your volunteers and present a poor witness to those you serve. Anticipate problems by making sure you have sufficient supplies to carry out the mission. Overprepare and ensure you have the necessary permissions to execute your plans if you are doing the outreach away from your church campus. Do everything you can not to waste time and to make the experience as positive and fulfilling as possible for the volunteers and those you serve.

Do's and Don'ts of Mission Projects

- Do study and get to know the community you want to reach. Don't assume everyone in the community is the same as the people within your church. Sometimes there is a distinct difference in who sits in the pew and who lives across the street. This is especially true when the church has been in the community a long time and the neighborhood has experienced a racial, social, or economic demographic change. Even if the people have many similarities, there may be a values or cultural difference that could be even more polarizing than ethnicity or economics. Conduct some market and field-based studies on your specific community. Thom Rainer has an invaluable tool on www.churchanswers.com/solutions/tools that could help.

- Do keep Jesus the main focus of the outreach project. While it is appropriate to highlight your church, make sure you do not promote your ministry over the person of Christ. Don't make your outreach seem like a gimmick to draw people to your church. You want to avoid seeming manipulative, disingenuous, and self-serving.
- Do develop relationships with the people you meet. Attempt to find ways to stimulate conversations with the people you serve. Even if it is only a few moments, look them in the eye and let them know you value them. Don't just hand out resources without some interpersonal connection.
- Do get authorization to operate the mission project. Alert neighbors of potential additional traffic in the neighborhood, excessive noise, or some other disturbance, especially if it will occur late into the evening. Don't forget to tell attendees not to block neighborhood driveways. The extra effort to forewarn residents of unusual church activity will foster goodwill with the community and abate future protests.
- Do include children and teenagers in outreach projects when possible. Don't underestimate the value of exposing them

to benevolent and altruistic causes while they are young, because it will pay generous dividends as they grow older.

- Do prepare your volunteers to present the gospel and share their personal testimony of faith with those they interact with. Don't assume everyone knows how. Arm each volunteer with a simple greeting to begin a spiritual conversation. A comment such as "Our church is doing this event to show our community the love of Christ in a tangible way, and we hope you feel the love" is a non-threatening way to spark a discussion. Rehearse other options in your training. Role-play potential scenarios.

- Do make sure you debrief with volunteers or key leadership after each event. Don't let a lot of time go by before talking about what went well, what went wrong, and what was confusing.

- Do seek to fund the program with church resources or outside sponsors. Don't do community events with the intention of the community bankrolling the outreach project. While it is appropriate to allow the community to purchase food or other items from food trucks and vendors, the primary purpose of the event should be funded by the church or sponsors.

- Do have a follow-up plan for decisions and contacts made at the event. Don't capture names on registration forms or offer an invitation to accept Christ without a plan for how the church will connect with respondents afterward. Too often, so much energy and time is given to plan and implementation, but very little effort is committed to follow up with attendees. Names remain in a box or file without a response. Put as much thought and energy in what happens after the event as you did in planning for the event.

- Do plan to have subsequent events or projects for the same people group to get a true picture of the success or failure of the outreach enterprise. Don't make a full assessment of whether something you tried worked or not until you have been able to connect and reconnect for a set period of time with that target people group or community. Outreach takes time and consistency before people will trust you and open their hearts and lives. One-time, big-event projects often do not have a significant long-term impact on a community.
- Do let prayer undergird all you do. Don't underestimate its power to tear down strongholds and the spiritual resistance that exists in the community you desire to reach.
- Do share with the congregation the success stories and life change experienced by those impacted by the church's outreach efforts. Don't leave members out. Use the church's website and publications, bulletins, announcements, and public testimony to communicate what God has done. You will inspire others to join you personally, financially, and with their prayers. You'll need all the help you can get!

Twenty-One Outreach Ideas That Can Make a Difference

1. The Outreach Challenge: Three to five teams consisting of five to ten members each are given $100 to $1,000 per team to come up with creative ways to use the resources to plan, implement, and report on the results of an outreach project they design. The team has thirty to sixty days to complete the task and to present to the church at a special service how they used the funds and how it benefited the recipients. The congregation or a special judging team (in the style of a television competition

show) will award the team they think used the funds the best. Ultimately, there are no losers because each team has touched many lives. This is just an imaginative way to get the church excited about missions, identify outreach leaders, and in some cases, to launch a ministry idea that may continue after the challenge is complete.

2. Arrange a technology support day for seniors in the community or residents of a nursing home. Have teens and young adults work with senior adults to teach them about tech issues with their phones, computers, tablets, or televisions.

3. When public schools have teacher workdays, the church can provide a youth fun day for students at the church. This program should be open to the community and advertised at the local school where parents can register their children. This is an excellent way to introduce your church to families in the community and helps your youth pastor and leaders to develop relationships with kids outside the church.

4. Using the professionals in your church or your trusted partners, host financial and career counseling; interview and résumé coaching; and grief, divorce, and mental health support groups. Following the global pandemic, governmental agencies are not able to meet the demand and are looking to partner with churches.

5. Organize a prayer station at a local mall or grocery store parking lot and offer prayer to passersby. Have prayer counselors and experienced mental health counselors on duty to meet the needs. This also works well in parks and alongside other events either at the church or at local community functions, such as football games or community festivals.

6. Provide breakfast or lunch for first responders, schoolteachers, hospital staff, and other service-oriented staff. Provide thank-you notes from the congregation and other items to encourage them. This works best if it is done consistently so that relationships with the staff can be established.

7. Open a free or sliding-scale counseling center at the church.

8. Conduct recovery ministry programs like Celebrate Recovery or some other Christ-centered services.

9. Reserve a few dates on the calendar for funerals for families who don't have a church home. Develop a relationship with the local mortician and let them know your church is open to assist at specific times for families who need that service.

10. Conduct an alternative to Halloween and open your church parking lot for a fall festival or trunk-or-treat.

11. Adopt a school or a number of schools in the community. Meet with the principal and find ways to address the needs of the students and staff.

12. Assign members to every school within a three-to-ten-mile radius of the church. Have them gather quarterly in the school's parking lot as a team and intercede for the school.

13. Host a parents'-night-out event for people who are fostering kids in your area. Work with the local county Child and Family Services to get a list of names and offer this service one Friday or Saturday night. Have activities and food at the church for the children and give the parents a gift card to go to dinner, attend a play, watch a movie, or go to a ball game.

14. Form a senior quilting or scrapbooking club, organize senior day trips with the local senior centers, or open your church for day activities with seniors in the community.

15. Work with the local hospitals and clinics to conduct community health screenings.

16. Conduct community cooking classes, newborn or parenting classes, premarital or newlywed counseling, exercise or aerobics sessions, and other programs that are all open to the community. Be sure to advertise them on community message boards, community newspapers, and on public church signage.

17. Host English as a second language courses and facilitate immigration support services.

18. Perform periodic free oil changes for single moms, hold free bike repair clinics, and host do-it-yourself clinics teaching basic home repair skills for your church and community.

19. If you are in a commercial or industrial area, offer to wash the windows for the local businesses two or three times a year. If your church is near a shopping mall or in a retail district, offer free gift wrapping at Christmas or special holidays.

20. Gather the youth in the fall and have them rake the leaves of neighbors, especially at the homes of the elderly or single moms. In the summer let them mow a few lawns.

21. Give out LED light bulbs or fire alarm batteries to persons in the community.

This is not an exhaustive list; there are thousands upon thousands of ideas, methods, and programs that could be employed to reach your community. My desire is simply to spark some creativity and inspire you to take what you've been given and watch Christ multiply it beyond your wildest expectations. There is no limit to the possibilities you and your church can accomplish.

You will be surprised by what God can do and who he will use to bring about the transformative change you seek. God used the little boy and his lunch to feed thousands. He used the disciples, who were physically tired and spiritually skeptical, to demonstrate his ability to meet needs. And he waits to surprise you as soon as you release what you have into his hands.

In our final moments together, I want to encourage you to begin to pray the prayer Jesus told us to pray as we seek to reach our community.

> Jesus traveled through all the towns and villages of that area, teaching in the synagogues and announcing the Good News about the Kingdom. And he healed every kind of disease and illness. When he saw the crowds, he had compassion on them because they were confused and helpless, like sheep without a shepherd. He said to his disciples, "The harvest is great, but the workers are few. So pray to the Lord who is in charge of the harvest; ask him to send more workers into his fields."[16]

We do not have to pray that there will be needs in people's lives for us to address. There are more than enough confused and helpless people all around us. They are truly sheep without a shepherd, and God has called us to go and rescue them with his Word and the freedom the gospel provides. Therefore, our prayer must be for laborers, workers, parents, students, retirees, young adults, singles, married couples, businessmen, teachers, politicians, servants, believers, and disciples to enter the fields, because THE HARVEST IS GREAT!

Notes

1. Tony Morgan, *The Unstuck Church: Equipping Churches to Experience Sustained Health* (Nashville: Thomas Nelson, 2017), 133.
2. Nona Jones, *From Social Media to Social Ministry: A Guide to Digital Discipleship* (Grand Rapids, MI: Zondervan, 2020), 15. Italics added.
3. NIV. Italics added.
4. Robert D. Lupton, *Toxic Charity: How Churches and Charities Hurt Those They Help (And How to Reverse It)* (New York: HarperOne, 2011), 147–148.
5. Kevin G. Harney, *Organic Outreach for Churches: Infusing Evangelistic Passion in Your Local Congregation* (Grand Rapids, MI: Zondervan, 2011), 119.
6. Dan Reiland, *Leadership Alone Isn't Enough: 40 Devotions to Strengthen Your Soul* (Bloomington, IN: WestBow Press, 2022).
7. Luke 6:32-36, NIV.
8. Jay Pathak and Dave Runyon, *The Art of Neighboring: Building Genuine Relationships Right Outside Your Door* (Grand Rapids, MI: Baker Books, 2012), 103.
9. Luke 2:49, NKJV.
10. Bob Whitesel, *Growth by Accident, Death by Planning: How Not to Kill a Growing Congregation* (Nashville: Abingdon Press, 2004), 17–25.
11. Alan Cooperman and Gregory A. Smith, "The Factors Driving the Growth of Religious 'Nones' in the U.S.," Pew Research Center, September 14, 2016, https://www.pewresearch.org/fact-tank/2016/09/14/the-factors-driving-the-growth-of-religious-nones-in-the-u-s/. Gregory A. Smith, "About Three-in-Ten U.S. Adults Are Now Religiously Unaffiliated," Pew Research Center, December 14, 2021,

https://www.pewresearch.org/religion/2021/12/14/about-three-in-ten-u-s
-adults-are-now-religiously-unaffiliated/.

12. John 4:3-4.

13. Rick Rusaw and Eric Swanson, *The Externally Focused Church* (Loveland,
CO: Group Publishing, 2004), 191.

14. Robert Lupton, *Toxic Charity: How Churches and Charities Hurt Those
They Help (And How to Reverse It)* (New York: HarperOne, 2011), 60–61.

15. Andrew Hall, "Spurgeon's 'Boiler Room' Secret of Success," *Northwest
Arkansas Democrat Gazette*, August 13, 2011.

16. Matthew 9:35-38.

About the Author

TYRONE BARNETTE is the senior pastor of Peace Baptist Church in Decatur, Georgia. He earned a master of divinity at Wesley Seminary at Indiana Wesleyan University and is currently pursuing his doctor of ministry degree in strategic leadership from New Orleans Baptist Theological Seminary. His beautiful wife and best friend, Tabitha, is his partner in ministry. God has graced them with three wonderful adult children: Joseph, Tallia, and Jonathan, and a granddaughter, Savannah.

If you liked this book, you'll want to get involved in

Church Equip!

Do you have a desire to learn more about serving God through your local church?

Would you like to see how God can use you in new and exciting ways?

Get your church involved in Church Equip, an online ministry designed to prepare church leaders and church members to better serve God's mission and purpose.

Check us out at **ChurchEquip.com**